The purpose of upholstery is to provide comfortable, durable, and good looking furniture.

NEW ESSENTIALS OF MODERN UPHOLSTERY

NEW ESSENTIALS OF MODERN UPHOLSTERY

HERBERT BAST

REVISION OF
ESSENTIALS OF MODERN UPHOLSTERY

THE BRUCE PUBLISHING COMPANY, NEW YORK
COLLIER-MACMILLAN LIMITED, LONDON

Library of Congress Catalog Card Number: 71-126189

THE BRUCE PUBLISHING COMPANY, NEW YORK

COLLIER-MACMILLAN CANADA, LTD., TORONTO, ONTARIO

Made in the United States of America

Introduction

This revised edition, entitled NEW ESSENTIALS OF MODERN UP-HOLSTERY, is intended to serve as a textbook in upholstery trades and to supply the necessary directions to a number of typical upholstering jobs. It should be helpful to retail upholstery or reupholstery shops, as well as to the average man or woman do-it-yourself enthusiast who wants to make or repair upholstered furniture. The book consists of the following sections, each updated with the latest available information:

Part I describes and illustrates the varied and numerous *tools, equipment,* and *supplies* used in upholstering. The addition of such items as the spring-end forming tool and the cushion filling machine makes the reader aware of the new technical equipment available to today's upholsterer.

Part II explains in detail many upholstery procedures, and makes practical applications of each of them. The subject is divided into *basic operations:* webbing, springs, stuffing, covering, finishing and trimming, cushioning, and furniture frames. Each operation is described and fully illustrated to make the step-by-step directions clear and easy to follow. While the techniques described are explained in terms of the jobs found in this section, they are the basic procedures and, therefore, applicable to upholstering other items of furniture regardless of style, shape, or size.

Also included within Part II, is background information about the upholstery *materials* to be used for each of the procedures. The origins and qualities of standard materials, such as cotton felt or kapok, as well as of newly developed products are fully discussed. The pupil who is interested in the subject of upholstery, either for practical purposes or for information, will find these sections of considerable interest, especially since he will be working with the materials. Like any other craftsman, the upholsterer should familiarize himself with the qualities and uses of all the materials he handles.

Part III supplies the directions for producing a variety of modern and imaginative upholstered items. The frames, which were selected for the jobs that are illustrated, are simple, and most of them can be made with the usual carpenter's hand tools. The new upholstery fillers, which are exclusively used for the jobs, provide freedom from dust and dirt, permitting anyone to do upholstery in the home. The instructions for performing these jobs will provide the student or the home practitioner with the opportunity to practice the techniques explained in Part II, and, at the same time, to produce a useful and attractive piece of furniture.

ACKNOWLEDGMENTS

The author wishes to thank the following firms for their assistance in compiling this book by contributing photographs and information for illustrations:

Blocksom and Company, Michigan City, Indiana
Broyhill Furniture Factories, Lenoir, North Carolina
Chandler Machine Company, Ayer, Massachusetts
Cox Furniture Company, Hickory, North Carolina
Firestone Industrial Products, Akron, Ohio
Gebhardt Supply Company, Milwaukee, Wisconsin
Gimbel Brothers, Custom Reupholstery Department, New York, New York
Hamilton Casco Company, Gallatin, Tennessee
Heminway and Bartlett Manufacturing Company, Watertown, Connecticut
Nettle Creek, Richmond, Virginia
Osborne Company, Harrison, New Jersey
Sackner Products, Grand Rapids, Michigan
Scotchgard, St. Paul, Minnesota
Seng Company, Chicago, Illinois
Shephard Company, Benton Harbor, Michigan
Tech Fab., St. Louis, Missouri
Western Filament Corporation, Glendale, California
Wolf Machine Company, Cincinnati, Ohio

TABLE OF CONTENTS

PART III. JOBS 149

1

TOOLS, EQUIPMENT, AND SUPPLIES

Figure 1. The finished product is the result of skillful use of tools, procedures, and materials.

Tools

The basic prerequisite for successful work in upholstery is a knowledge of the tools of the trade. The more important tools are illustrated and described in this chapter.

Upholsterer's Hammer (Figure 2)

The upholsterer's hammer has a head about 5½ inches long, with a face 5/16 to ½ inch in diameter. With a hammer of this shape, it is possible to tack in deep corners, and to tack on gimp without marring the woodwork.

Figure 2. Upholsterer's hammer.

Shears (Figure 3)

It is important that suitable shears be used, because most covering material is quite heavy and the shears are also used for cutting webbing, burlap, twine, etc. They should be of good quality and not less than 7 inches, preferably 10 inches long.

Figure 3. Upholsterer's shears.

Webbing Stretcher (Figure 4)

This tool is used to stretch webbing across the openings of furniture frames. It is padded on the end that is placed against the frame in order to prevent marring the finished woodwork. The use of the webbing stretcher is illustrated in Figure 35.

Figure 4. Webbing stretcher.

Upholsterer's Pin or Skewer (Figure 5)

This pin is used as a temporary basting for covers. It enables the upholsterer to get covers on straight and to obtain the firmness desired before sewing or tacking the covering. It is also used to pin up cushion openings before sewing.

These pins are obtainable in 3 or 3½ inch lengths. For some of the many uses for this pin, see Figures 72, 156, and 165.

Figure 5. Upholsterer's pin or skewer.

Ripping Tool (Figure 6)

This tool, used to remove tacks, is essential in repair work where old coverings are to be taken off.

Figure 6. Ripping tool for removing tacks.

Curved Needle (Figure 7)

The curved needle, which may be from 2 to 8 inches in circumference, is used to sew flat surfaces where it is impossible to use a straight needle, that is to say, where using a straight needle would mean reaching on the other side of the job to push the needle back. Large, heavy, curved needles are used for sewing stuffing to burlap and for sewing a stitched edge (Figure 75), whereas the smaller and finer needles are used for sewing on outsides.

Figure 7. Upholsterer's curved needle.

Straight Upholsterer's Needle (Figure 8)

Straight upholsterer's needles are available in 6 to 12 inch lengths. They are used to sew springs to webbing, stuffing to burlap, etc. The double points permit sewing down and up without turning the needle around. One of the many uses for this needle is shown in Figure 74.

Figure 8. Upholsterer's straight needle.

Stuffing Regulator (Figure 9)

The regulator, which may be from 6 to 10 inches long, is used to even out irregularities in stuffing. This operation should be performed while stuffing with a temporary muslin cover before the top cover is put on, because regulating through a top cover is likely to leave holes in the fabric. Another use for the regulator is shown in Figure 105,

Figure 9. Stuffing regulator.

Tack and Staple Remover (Figure 10)

The tack and staple remover is made of forged steel with a wooden handle. It removes tacks and staples in a hurry.

Figure 10. Tack and staple remover.

Spring-Bender Tool (Figure 11)

The spring-bender tool is used to get the precise arc, angle, or curve desired in no-Sag springs. It has a chrome-plated iron head with slots to fit into the loops of the spring. The handles are made of sturdy, translucent, easy-grip plastic.

To use the spring-bender tool, simply hold one bender in each hand and exert pressure in opposite directions to get the curve desired.

To undo a previously made arc, merely apply reverse pressure to its original shape. See Figure 12.

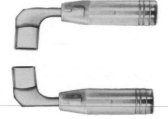

Figure 11. Spring-bender tool.

Figure 12. Use of the spring-bender tool.

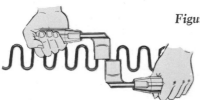

Equipment

Benches or Trestles (Figure 13)

It is not absolutely necessary for the craftsman to have a set of benches or trestles for assembling or upholstering one piece of furniture, because a padded table can be used. However, if the work involves several pieces, it would be advisable to get two trestles on which it can be supported.

Trestles should be light enough for easy handling and at the same time strong enough to accommodate all kinds and sizes of furniture. They should be constructed so that the furniture will

Figure 13. Padded bench or trestle.

not slip off, and they should have either a pad on top or a stuffed roll edge all around the top. (For the construction of a stuffed roll edge see Figure 66). The pad or roll edge prevents marring the legs or other finished surfaces on a piece of furniture when it is laid on its back or side. Trestles are usually made 36 inches long, 30 inches high, with the top board 8 inches wide.

Sewing Machine (Figure 14)

A sewing machine to be used for sewing upholstery covering should be of sturdy construction. Many upholstery coverings are heavy in texture. Others are made with rubberized backing, and in some types of construction, welt is inserted between seams which makes it necessary to sew through four thicknesses. It is important, therefore, to set the stitching adjustment on "large," so that the cover will feed through the machine. Then, too, it is best to use a heavy-duty thread with the proper size needle for this thread. Also, when sewing over welt seams, it is advisable to work

Figure 14. Completely equipped upholstery sewing machine.

8

the sewing machine slowly, turning the wheel by hand rather than trying to force the needle through at high speed. This will save many bent or broken needles.

For machine-sewing upholstery covers where a welt is inserted between the seams, a welt foot, or so-called zipper foot, is necessary (see Figures 115 & 116). Most of the newer sewing machines include this zipper foot with their attachments but the older models did not. This zipper foot may be purchased for various kinds of sewing machines in most sewing machine centers or department stores.

When purchasing a sewing machine for upholstery repair, commercial, or production work, make certain that the machine is intended for upholstery sewing and that it is purchased from a reliable and established firm, so that service and parts may be obtained. Also, make sure of the following features:

- Ample clearance under the pressure foot to permit doing a job with light as well as heavy material.
- A reverse stitch mechanism to back-tack seam ends and to reinforce the strain areas.
- A walking foot which prevents either the top or bottom of the material from gathering.
- A welt foot attachment which is a must for upholstery sewing.

Button Machine (Figure 15)

It is not necessary to purchase a button machine for upholstering or reupholstering a piece of furniture that may require only a few upholstery buttons. Most department stores and upholstery shops will make covered buttons to order in various sizes. However, a button machine is a profitable investment as well as a great convenience in upholstery, furniture, and interior decorating shops.

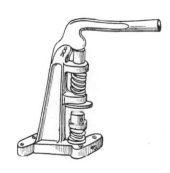

With this device, upholstery-covered buttons can be made in various sizes and styles. For upholstery, the No. 22 size is most generally used. Button molds come in four types: (*a*) tuft, (*b*) loop, (*c*) tack, (*d*) clinch (Figure 16). This machine also can be used for attaching snap fasteners, eyelets, grommets, ventilators, washers, etc., by adding the necessary attachments.

The operation of a button machine is simple and directions for making buttons come with the machine. For making larger buttons by hand, see Figure 107.

Figure 16. Four types of buttons:
(a) tuft, (b) loop, (c) tack,
(d) clinch.

Cutting Machine (Figure 17)

The electric cutting machine is a "must" in any upholstery shop, especially where sponge rubber, or polyfoam is used extensively. It will cut straight lines as well as rounded corners or curves, depending upon the shape and size of the cushion or pillow.

Figure 17. Cutting machine.

Cushion Filling Machine (Figure 18)

This foot-operated cushion filler has become a country-wide standard in the upholstering trade. By using a special pan arrangement, the range of cushion widths is increased considerably. Such a feature is necessary in order to fill all of the cushion sizes now encountered in upholstery shops.

An "electromatic" cushion filler may also be obtained for any size shop where it is desirable or essential to reduce the manual labor required to operate a foot-lever filler.

Figure 18. Cushion filling machine.

11

Spring-end forming tool (Figure 19)

This entirely new and practical device is used for crimping all sizes of open-end coil springs, as well as finishing the ends of zig-zag type wire in all gauges and widths.

Crimping the open end of coil springs to be used in the leading edges of chair and sofa foundations has always been a makeshift operation—usually done with a length of pipe at the risk of skinned knuckles.

Zig-zag type wire, cut to length from stock coils, must have the open ends reversed to restrain the securing clips, and to allow the unfinished ends to sit properly on the frame. With no alterations or change over, this tool will make proper and uniform crimps in this type of wire.

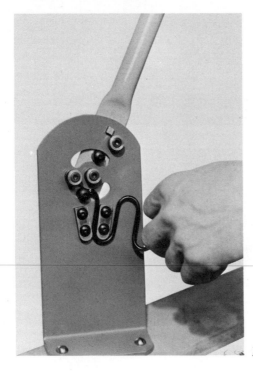

Figure 19. Spring-end forming tool.

Supplies

Upholstery Tacks (Figure 20)

    Upholstery tacks have a flat head and can be purchased in a large assortment of sizes (from 1 to 24 ounces) to meet a variety of demands. The size of the tack used in upholstery is determined

Figure 20.
Upholstery tacks.

OZ.	1	$1\frac{1}{2}$	2	$2\frac{1}{2}$	3
SIZE	$\frac{3}{16}''$	$\frac{3\frac{1}{2}}{16}''$	$\frac{4}{16}''$	$\frac{5}{16}''$	$\frac{6}{16}''$

SIZE	$\frac{10}{16}''$	$\frac{9}{16}''$	$\frac{8}{16}''$	$\frac{7}{16}''$
OZ.	10	8	6	4

SIZE	$\frac{11}{16}''$	$\frac{12}{16}''$	$\frac{13}{16}''$	$\frac{14}{16}''$	$\frac{15}{16}''$
OZ.	12	14	16	18	20

13

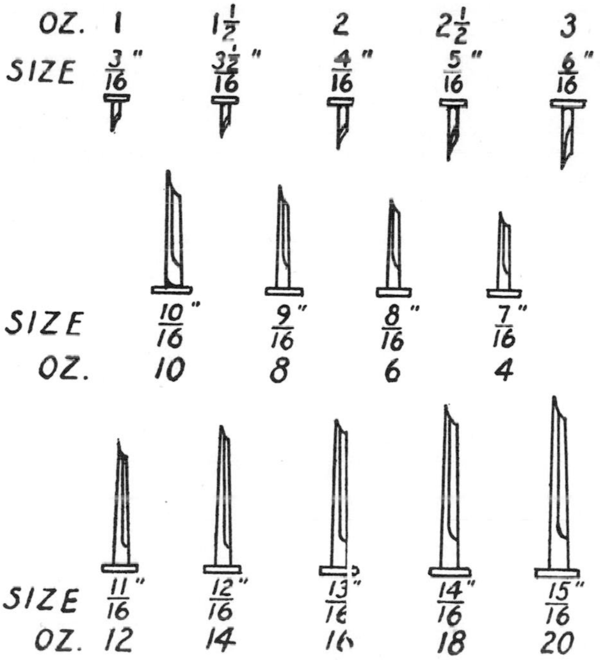

by the thickness of the covering, the thickness of the frame, and by the weight to be supported. When tacking webbing to a seat frame, a larger tack is required, and when tacking it to the back frame, a smaller tack is used.

For upholstery, the tacks most commonly used are the 3-, 4-, 6-, 8-, 10-, and 12-ounce sizes. Upholstery tacks are sold in 1/4- and 1-pound papers, 5- and 25-pound boxes, and 100-pound kegs.

Gimp Tacks (Figure 21)

Gimp tacks have a small round head. They are used to tack cloth gimp to furniture (Figure 122) and are frequently used to tack outside coverings to backs and arms. Gimp tacks can be obtained in sizes from 2 to 8 ounces, and are sold in 1/4- and 1-pound papers and 5- and 25-pound boxes.

Figure 21. Gimp tacks.

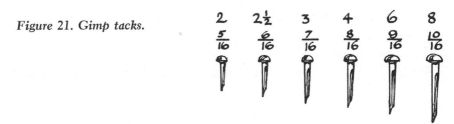

Flathead Wood Screws (Figure 22)

Flathead wood screws are used on frames, especially the upholstered type, where the wood is covered (Figures 175 & 191). They are also used to fasten corner blocks (Figure 184). This type of wood screw is available in various lengths and diameters.

Figure 22. Flathead wood screws.

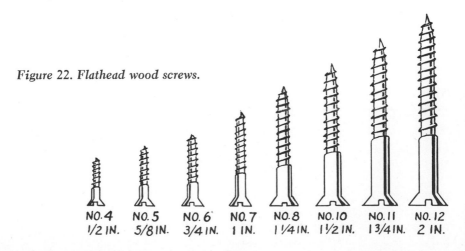

14

Wood Dowels (Figures 23 and 24)

Wood dowels are used to join furniture frames, especially frames where the joint is exposed (Figures 183 & 184).

They are usually made of birch, and can be obtained in 3 foot lengths with diameters varying from ⅛ to 1 inch. This type of dowel is cut to length to suit the requirements of the job.

Wood dowels are also supplied with a spiraled groove cut into them (Figure 24). These dowels are cut to a length of 2 inches and range in diameter from ⅛ to ⅝ inch. The holding power of spiraled grooved dowels is far superior to that of plain dowels because the grooves permit the glue to spread throughout the joint. On the other hand, the smooth plain dowels, especially when fitted too tightly, will not permit glue to adhere to the sides of the dowel when they are driven into place.

Figure 23. Wood dowels.

Figure 24. A grooved dowel.

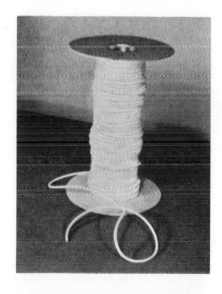

Figure 25. A roll of welt cord.

Welt Cord (Figure 25)

Welt cord is inserted between 1½-inch strips of material which are then sewn between seams in the upholstery coverings. (For cutting and sewing welt see page 89). Welt is used extensively in upholstery and slip-cover making.

Welt cord is sold in most department stores by the yard. For production work, welt cord can be purchased in rolls of 500 yards and in thicknesses of ⅛, 5/32, and ¼ inch. The 5/32-inch size is most commonly used.

15

Thread

Upholstery thread is made from cotton, linen, nylon, and other synthetic materials. It is available in a wide variety of colors that match the many shades found in upholstery fabrics.

A recent development in threads is a new monofilamentous, transparent thread for sewing all upholstery fabrics regardless of color. Its many advantages make this new thread a very practical and useful supply to have on hand. Because the thread is transparent, the need to stock a vast variety of threads and then to change from color to color as the fabric demands is eliminated. It is a versatile thread which can be used for machine or hand sewing, and it increases the strength of seams because it will not rot, fade, mildew, fray or shrink. This thread also resists deterioration caused by exposure to household detergents and alkalies.

Casters (Figures 26, 27, & 28)

Since most overstuffed furniture is built with short, heavy legs, or, in many cases, no legs at all, it is a practical idea to attach casters thereby increasing mobility and protecting the flooring. The greatest problem with casters, however, is that the wheel on the caster does not always readily turn in the direction that it was intended to turn. The development of a new type of caster whose wheel swivels instantly has eliminated this problem.

The large selection of these casters available enables the buyer to choose a size, style, and finish compatible with the design of his furniture. Since these casters may be purchased with sockets or with legs attached, they fit practically any frame construction regardless of weight be it an ottoman, a heavy chair, a davenport, a bed, or a T.V. set.

Figure 26. Casters with legs attached.

Figure 27. Socket type casters.

Figure 28. Casters on heavy furniture.

A knowledge of the fundamental processes of upholstering is, of course, essential to any upholsterer. In the following section, all of the basic procedures necessary for a complete upholstery job from webbing through finishing and frame construction are explained in sequential order.

Because it is equally important for the upholsterer to understand the materials with which he is working, the sources and manufacture of such materials as webbing, burlap, and stuffing are also included.

Procedure 1.   Webbing

Jute

Upholstery webbing is made entirely of jute fiber. The jute fiber, from which both burlap and webbing are made, is the bast or woody fiber of plants (Figure 29) that are grown in India, mostly in Bengal and the district around Calcutta. The plants are annuals that are sown in the spring and harvested in the fall. They grow to a height of from 10 to 15 feet. When exported, the fibers are in a state ready to be handled by machinery.

The city of Calcutta, besides exporting a large amount of fiber, is the largest center in the world for the manufacture of burlap which is made entirely of jute fiber.

The preparation of the fiber from the jute plant is a rather simple operation. The plant is usually cut while in bloom, and the stalks are freed from leaves, seed capsules, and so on. They are then retted (rotted) by steeping in a sluggish stream of water. After a few days the fiber becomes disintegrated, and the retted stalks are pressed and scutched (beaten) to separate the fibers from the soft parts. The fiber so obtained is remarkably pure and free from other tissue. These prepared fibers are usually from 4 to 8 feet long.

The ends of the plants and short waste fibers, known to the trade as "jute butts" or "jute cuttings," are used in the manufacture of wrapping paper.

The processes at the jute mills are similar to those used at cotton mills, although the machinery is heavier since the jute fiber

21

Figure 29. Detail of the jute plant.

Figure 30. Upholstery webbing in a 72 yard roll.

is much coarser than cotton fiber. The jute is first put through a combing process to make the fibers lie flat and parallel to each other; then it undergoes a spinning process, making a thread strong enough to stand the strain of the loom in weaving.

Because the jute fiber has very little elasticity, it is especially adapted to upholstery use. When properly tacked and stretched, jute webbing will stay in place and preserve the shape of the cover for a long period of time.

The standard widths of webbing are, 3, 3½, and 4 inches. The 3½ inch width is the most popular. Some concerns use the 3 inch width for backs and arms, but it is never advisable to use the 3 inch width for seats. Most manufacturers use the 3½ inch width throughout, because they then have to carry only one size in stock, and the upholsterers need not change from one size of webbing to another. The units, as shipped to the upholstery trade from the mills, are bales containing 24 rolls each, with 72 yards of webbing to the roll. This gives 12 gross yards to the bale.

Upholstery webbing may also be purchased by the yard at many large department stores or at upholstery supply dealers.

22

AMOUNT AND LOCATION OF WEBBING

The necessary amount of webbing is determined either by the size of the opening in the frame or by the weight the webbing will carry. The seat in a chair or davenport should contain more strips of webbing than should the back.

Where springs are used in seats, it is advisable to have at least one strip of webbing each way for each row of springs.

1. *To Locate Position of Webbing*

Locate the middle of the front, back, and sides of the frame. Should there be an odd number of strips, it is best to put the center web in first, and space the others on each side. If the number of strips is even, one half of the strips will be placed to one side of the middle mark, and the other half on the other side.

Figure 31. Proper spacing of webbing in davenport seat.

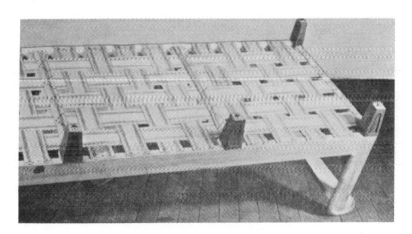

On davenports and chairs with a spring-edge seat, it is advisable to have the front cross strip of webbing close to the front of the frame because the front row of springs in this type of construction must be placed directly against the inside of the frame. The rear strip of cross webbing may be some distance from the rear of the seat frame since the springs in this type of seat should not be placed against the rear of the frame.

23

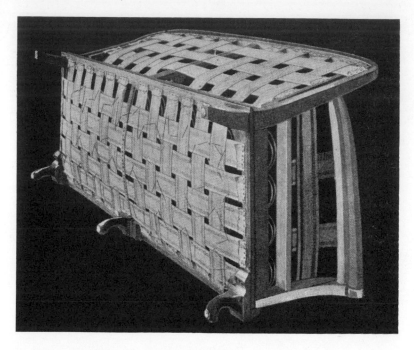

Figure 32. Webbing correctly positioned.

2. To Determine the Amount of Webbing to Be Used

Measure the size of the opening, front to back. Add 3 inches to each strip for turning over 1½ inches on each end. Multiply the length in inches of one strip by the number of strips required. Apply the same method to determine the amount of webbing to be used crosswise.

Questions

1. On chairs or davenports with a spring edge, why is it necessary to have the front cross strip of webbing close to the front of the frame?
2. How much webbing will be required for a davenport seat 6 feet long and 2½ feet deep, using 12 strips front to back and 5 strips across?
3. What is the best way to position webbing when there are an odd number of strips? an even number of strips?

TACKING AND STRETCHING WEBBING

Webbing is stretched across the opening as a foundation for all the work that is to follow. The frame of the opening must be strong enough to carry the tension strain of the webbing and the weight to be supported. The amount and quality of the webbing will depend upon the type of work to be done.

When possible, webbing is tacked in the front and stretched to the rear, for two reasons. Some pieces of furniture have a partially obstructed front surface which would not permit the use of the stretcher in front. In this case, the webbing may be tacked on the inside of the frame, in front, and stretched to the rear with a stretcher. The second reason for stretching webbing to the rear is to avoid marring the front wood rail of some pieces of furniture.

When stretching, gauge the strain properly to the strength of the frame and to the elasticity of the webbing. The webbing must not be stretched to the breaking point, but must be capable of giving slightly under the pressure of use, and, at the same time, be taut enough to prevent bulging when the springs are tied down.

When the strips of webbing are stretched in a straight line, they serve as a guide for sewing the springs in a straight line.

The size of the tacks to be used will depend upon the thickness and quality of the frame. The tacks are staggered in the webbing. If all the tacks were placed in a row, they might split the frame (Figure 33).

Figure 33. Webbing properly tacked.

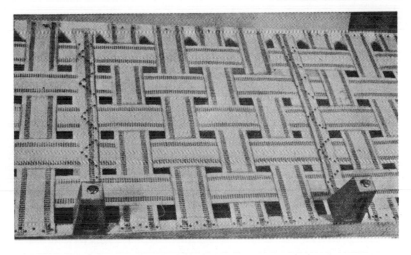

All cross webbings are interlaced to make a firm foundation, and to prevent sagging of any webs not stretched as tightly as the others.

Tools and Equipment

Upholstering hammer; webbing stretcher; shears

Materials

Webbing; tacks

Procedure

1. *Place the Furniture in Position for Webbing.*

2. *Locate the Position for the Strips of Webbing.*
   This will be determined by the number of strips to be used. (To determine position and amount of webbing, see pages 23 and 24.)

3. *Open the Roll of Webbing.*
   Release the outside and center ends, so that both ends of the roll may be worked with at the same time. When two rolls of webbing are available, it is best to release the outside and center ends of each roll, since this will permit working with four ends of webbing. The webbing ends can then be used as a spacing guide (Figure 34).

4. *Tack the First or Free End.*
   Fold the end back about 1½ inches, and tack through both thicknesses, staggering the tacks.

5. *Tack the Second or Stretched End.*
   - Place the padded end of the stretcher against the outside of the frame. The stretcher is padded so as not to mar any finished woodwork.
   - Hook the nail end of the stretcher in the webbing, and pull down (Figure 35).
   - Tack the webbing to the frame.
   - Cut the webbing off about 1½ inches from the tacks.
   - Fold the webbing back over the tacks, and tack again, staggering the tacks with those previously placed.

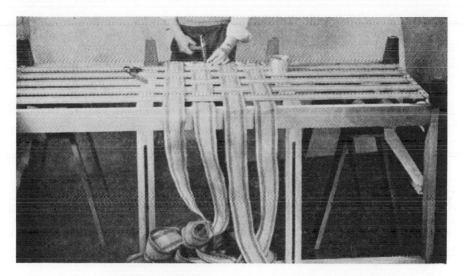

Figure 34. Using two rolls of webbing.

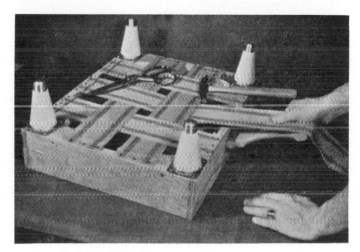

*Figure 35. Using a
webbing stretcher.*

Questions

1. Why is webbing stretched across the opening of a frame?
2. What will determine the size of tacks to be used in fastening webbing?
3. What is the meaning of "staggering tacks"?
4. Why are tacks staggered?
5. Why are webbings interlaced?
6. Why is it good practice to tack webbing to the front of the frame and stretch it to the rear?
7. Why should webbing be stretched in a straight line?

27

Procedure 2. Springs

Springs

After the webbing is in place, the next step is the selection and placement of springs. There are various sizes, wire gauges, and types of springs used in upholstery. Each has a definite place and use depending on the resiliency required.

Upholstery Springs

Upholstery springs are usually open at both ends. One end of the spring is bent toward the center when the spring is in place; this end should be on top. The tip is bent down so as not to wear a hole in the burlap and thus permit the stuffing to fall into the springs.

Upholstery springs (Figure 36) are made of 9- to 11-gauge wire, and are used in furniture seats. They may be 4 to 14 inches in height.

Upholstery springs may be either soft spring or stiff spring. The soft spring has a wide center, and the stiff spring has a narrow center.

Figure 36. Upholstery spring.

Pillow Springs

Pillow springs (Figure 37) are *not* used in pillows as the name implies. They are made of relatively fine 12- to 15-gauge wire, and are used in backs of furniture. These springs are usually knotted at both ends, so there is no definite top or bottom of the spring.

Figure 37. Knotted pillow spring.

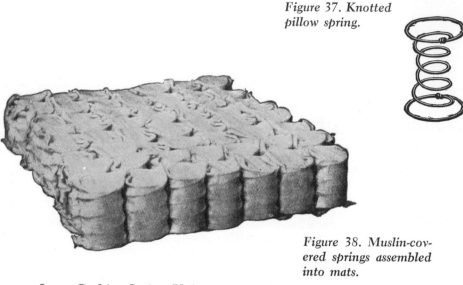

Figure 38. Muslin-covered springs assembled into mats.

Inner-Cushion-Spring Unit

Inner-cushion-spring units (Figure 38) are used inside of the loose cushions that are popular on overstuffed furniture. These sets of inner springs are made up of small springs, about 3½ inches high and about 3 inches in diameter. Each spring is sewed into separate rows of pockets of either muslin (Figure 39) or burlap. The rows of pockets can then be assembled for various odd sizes and shapes.

Figure 39. Muslin-covered cushion springs.

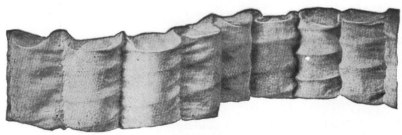

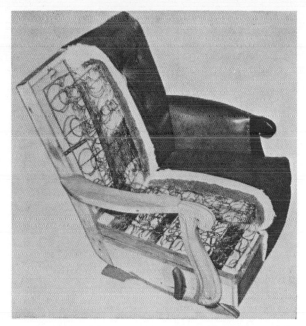

Figure 40. Construction springs made to fit a platform rocker.

Construction Springs

Because construction springs are primarily used by manufacturers of upholstered furniture for production work, they are made to order in quantities. Construction springs may be had to fit any particular size or shape furniture, with a wire gauge to suit the resiliency desired (Figure 40).

Nonsagging Springs

Nonsagging springs (also called hairpin or zigzag springs) are made in a continuous serpentine strip (Figure 41). These strips can be cut into the desired lengths. They also may be purchased cut to specified lengths with the ends bent, ready to attach. Nonsagging springs are made in 7- to 12-gauge wire. The heavier gauges, 7 to 9, are used in seats, while the lighter gauges, 10 to 12, are used in backs.

When using this type of spring, it is necessary to nail the ends onto the frame with clips made for this purpose, and to use helical springs between the rows.

Figure 41. Strips of springs cut to size.

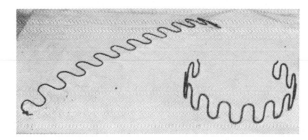

Twines

There are 3 kinds of twines generally used for tying the springs. They differ according to weight and strength as well as to use.

Spring Twine

Spring twine (Figure 42) is used for tying down heavy upholstery springs in seats. While there are various qualities of spring twine, a good quality should be selected, since a poor twine may break or wear out and thus ruin the seat in a short time. Spring twine comes in 1-pound balls with six balls to a package.

Jute Twine

Jute twine (Figure 43) is softer and lighter in weight than spring twine. It is used for tying down pillow springs which are used in backs of furniture. Jute twine is also used for wrapping and packing purposes and comes in 1-pound balls with six balls to a package.

Flax (stitching) Twine

Flax twine (Figure 44) is used for sewing springs to webbing, sewing stitched edges, fastening buttons, and in all kinds of hand sewing by upholsterers. This twine comes in ½-pound balls with six balls to a package.

Figure 42. Spring twine.   *Figure 43. Jute twine.*   *Figure 44. Flax twine.*

NUMBER AND SIZE OF SPRINGS

After the webbing has been tacked in place and the piece of furniture has been turned over on its feet, the next step is to select the proper springs and to determine the number required. The size of the opening will indicate how many springs to use. They should be equally distributed, so that each spring will give freely under pressure without coming in contact with the others. If they are crammed too closely in the center, the result will be a hard seat. If they are too far apart, the result will be a weak seat, which will allow one sitting down hard to strike bottom. To remedy the latter condition, use springs of a smaller size and use more of them.

The size of the springs is governed by the resiliency required in the finished seat or back. The less they are compressed in tying, the greater the resiliency; and since the resiliency can never be greater than that permitted by the twine, the higher the tops of the springs are above the frame, the more resilient the seat. In seats, the top of the tied-down springs should never, under ordinary circumstances, be less than 3 inches above the frame. This will permit the spring to be depressed without taking up all the slack in the spring twine. If the springs are tied lower than 3 inches above the boxing, the twine and burlap will soon tear away from the frame and permit the stuffing to fall into the springs. Where it is necessary to tie the springs lower than 3 inches above the frame, the twine should be brought to the bottom of the inside of the frame, and this burlap should be left loose enough so it will not tear away when one is sitting on the seat.

The weakest part of the spring is the waist or center. A spring with a wide center is softer than one with a narrow center, and, if the spring is too narrow at this point, it may become weakened and useless.

Questions

1. What will determine the size of springs to use on a given job?
2. What will be the result if too many or too large springs are used?
3. What will be the result if too few or too small springs are used?
4. What should be the minimum height of the springs above the frame after they have been tied down? Why?

PLACING AND FASTENING SPRINGS

1. *Placing Springs*

On open springs, one end or tip is bent toward the center, when the spring is in place; this end should be on top. The tip is bent down so as not to wear a hole in the burlap and thus permit the stuffing to fall in the springs.

Care should be taken that springs stand directly in line, otherwise it will be difficult to tie them down. Where a spring edge is desired, the bottom of the springs should be placed directly against the wood frame, and the top of the springs bent outward even with the outer edge of the frame.

2. *Fastening Springs to Webbing*

When the springs are placed in their proper position, the next step is fastening them to the webbing. There is only one method of fastening, and that is to sew them down. They must be sewed down tight, or they will wear out the twine and fall over. Care must be taken that the springs do not move from their proper positions during the process of sewing.

Tools and Equipment

Shears; needle; hammer

Materials

Webbing; springs; stitching twine; tacks or staples

Procedure

1. *Locate Position of Springs.*

The position will be determined by the number of springs to be used.

Figure 45. Springs sewn to webbing.

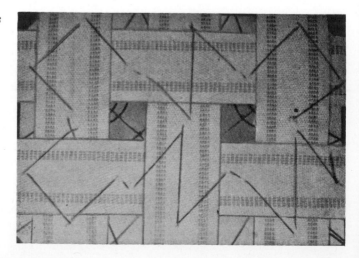

2. *Sew Springs to Webbing.*
Use four stitches to each spring. Plan the stitches so that the last stitch will be at the nearest point to the next spring.

3. *Springs Fastened to Webbing with Klinch-it Fasteners.*
Klinch-it fasteners are one of the biggest improvements in upholstery. These spring fasteners clip springs solidly to the webbing construction, leaving the springs firmly in place. Four equally spaced fastener staples should be used on each spring.

Because it is faster than hand sewing, the Klinch-it fastener method cuts down production costs. It is now used by virtually all leading manufacturers of upholstered furniture, and by upholsterers who find it practical for repair and service work.

Figure 46. Springs fastened to webbing with klinch-it fastener.

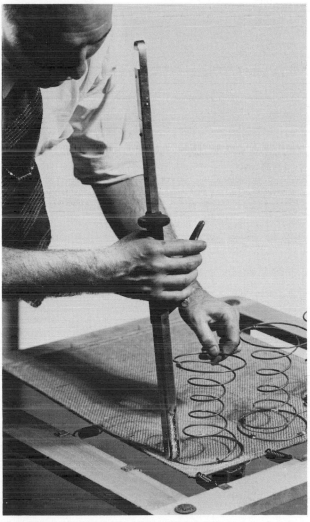

4. *Fastening Springs to Wood.*

On furniture frames with wood slats or on a solid wood base, there are two methods of fastening springs. One is with ordinary staples, the other with upholsterer's tacks placed next to each side of the bottom coil. The heads of the tacks will prevent the spring from shifting (Figure 47). Regardless of which method

 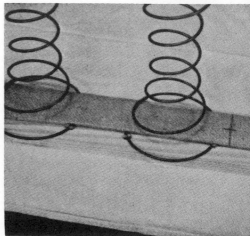

Figure 47. Springs tacked to wood slats with upholsterer's tacks.

Figure 48. Silencer strip in place to prevent rattling.

is used to fasten springs to wood, it will be necessary to place some sort of silencer below the unfastened coils to prevent rattling when the depressed coil strikes the wood. The silencer material may be a strip of webbing, burlap, or other waste material (Figure 48).

Questions
1. How is the top of an open spring determined?
2. Why must springs stand directly in line?
3. How are front springs placed for a spring edge?
4. In sewing springs to webbing, how many stitches should be taken to each spring?
5. How should these stitches be placed?
6. How are the positions of the springs located?
7. Name two methods of fastening springs to wood.
8. On springs fastened to wood, what is required underneath the lower coil? Why?

TYING SPRINGS TO HEIGHT

When the springs have been fastened in position, the next step is to tie them down. The life of the furniture depends upon the condition of the springs, which, in turn, depends chiefly upon the manner in which they have been tied. Care must be taken that the springs stand straight and do not slip on the twine when tied down.

Tools and Equipment

Hammer; shears

Materials

Spring twine; tacks

Procedure

1. *Measuring Spring Twine.*
   For round or stuffed seats in chairs or stools, hold the twine over the first row of springs, allowing about 2 inches to each spring, for knots.

   For flat seats, especially where loose cushions are used, allow enough twine to make a return tie at each end. The return tie must be long enough to go over the top of the first spring, and be tied to the top of the second spring.

2. *Cutting Spring Twine.*
   Cut as many pieces of twine as there are rows of springs, so that all the pieces of twine will be of equal length, and all may be tacked on one end before tying the springs.

3. *Fastening Spring Twine to the Frame.*
   - Place two slip tacks, ½ inch apart, in line with each row of springs. This is especially necessary where there is a strain in pulling down the springs.
   - For round or stuffed seats, where no return twine is necessary, fasten the end of each twine around the two tacks and drive the tacks down.
   - On flat seats where a return twine is used, fasten the twine around the two tacks at the proper place to allow for the return twine, and drive the tacks down. This provides two

37

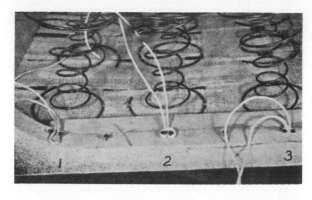

Figure 49. Proper method of fastening spring twine to a frame.

lengths of twine to work with at each row of springs—the first or long twine, and the short return twine (Figure 49).

4. Tying Springs to Height—Round Seats.
- On round or stuffed seats, knot the twine to both top coils of each spring.
- Loop the twine around one of the tacks, pull down to the desired height, and drive this tack down. Loop the twine around the second tack, and drive this tack down.
- Proceed in the same manner in each row until all rows of springs have been tied down to the desired height (Figure 50).

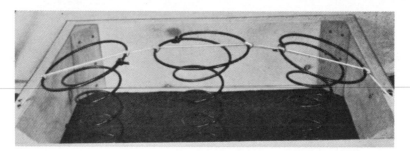

Figure 50. Springs tied down for a round seat.

5. Tying Springs to Height—Flat Seat.
- For flat seats, especially where loose cushions are used, loop the first or long twine around the top coils of each spring, omitting the outer coil at each end.
- Loop the twine around one of the tacks, pull down to the desired height, and drive this tack down. Loop the twine around the second tack, and drive this tack down. This looping of the

38

first twine permits each spring to be moved in a straight line after it has been pulled down to the desired height.

- Follow with the return twine from each end, draw the outer coil down even with the middle spring, knot the return twine over each loop, and finally fasten it to the middle spring. The knotting of the return twine over each loop will now hold the spring in its permanent position (Figure 51).

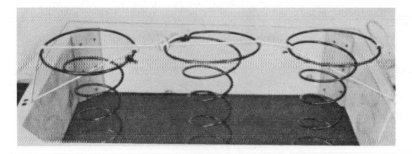

Figure 51. Springs tied down for a flat seat with a return twine.

Questions

1. In tying springs to height, why should the first twine be looped?
2. What is a return twine?
3. Why must return twine be knotted?
4. In measuring spring twine, how much allowance should be made for knots?

MAKING A SPRING EDGE

A spring edge with a wire attached to the front is very popular on most overstuffed davenports and chairs. This type of front affords resilience across the entire front of the seat.

With the spring edge, it will be necessary to bend the top coils of the front springs outward so that the front top coil of the spring will extend even with the outer edge of the frame. This will permit tying the front spring down without leaning forward. Then, too, it will be necessary to have the bottom coil set directly against the inside of the frame.

Tools and Equipment

Hammer; shears; pliers

Materials

Spring twine; tacks

Procedure

1. *Bending Springs.*
   Bend the top coils of the front springs outward, so they will extend even with the outside of the frame. This permits the wire edge to be even with the outside of the frame and, at the same time, allows the front springs to stand almost straight (Figure 52).

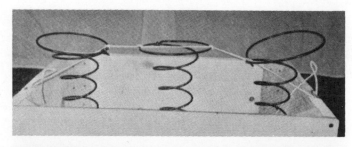

Figure 52. Springs pulled down for a spring edge.

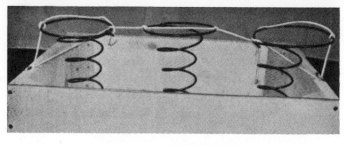

Figure 53. Rear and front return twines tied down.

2. *Measuring the Spring Twine.*
   - Hold the twine over the row of springs front to back, allowing about 2 inches to each spring for knots.
   - Determine the length of return twine required at the rear, and allow enough twine to reach over the top of the front spring and back down to the frame (Figures 52 & 53).

3. *Fastening the Spring Twine to the Frame.*
   - Fasten the twine to the rear of the frame (Figure 49) allowing enough for the return twine. This process provides two twines to work with at each row of springs—the first, or long twine and a short return twine.
   - Knot the first, or long twine to the top coils of each spring, omitting the outer coils at the rear and at the front.

Care must be taken in tying the knot to the front spring so that the top coil of the front spring will extend even with the outer edge of the frame after the front top coil is tied down (Figure 53).

4. *Tying Down the Springs.*
   - Pull the springs down to the desired height.
   - Tack the twine firmly to the front.
   - Knot the rear return twine to the outer coil of the rear spring, pulling the outer end of the spring down even with the center spring.

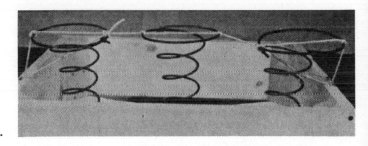

Figure 54. Springs properly tied down for a spring edge.

   - Knot the front return twine to the outer coil of the front spring (Figure 54).
   - Knot the front return twine over the knot which was used to pull the spring down.
   - Knot this twine at the coil nearest the top of the frame (Figure 54).

Questions

1. What is the purpose of a spring edge?
2. In what position are the front springs in a spring edge?
3. Where is the bottom coil of the front spring set?
4. How much twine is allowed to each spring for knots?

BENDING AND FASTENING WIRE TO SPRING EDGE

A wire edge must be bent to the exact shape of the frame, and to be durable, must be properly attached to the springs. The wire must be bent to its proper shape before being attached to the springs, otherwise the twine may be loosened while bending the wire. A No. 9 spring wire is commonly used for this purpose.

41

Tools and Equipment

Shears; pliers; hammer

Materials

Spring wire; twine

Procedure

1. *Bending Wire to a Sharp Corner.*
The wire may be held and bent with pliers, or run through a piece of pipe of small diameter and bent over the edge (Figure 55).

2. *Bending Wire to a Curve.*
Lay the wire on a block of wood, and tap the wire with a hammer until the desired shape has been formed (Figure 56).

3. *Fastening Wire.*
Fasten the wire to the springs with stitching twine, beginning in the center and interlacing, first to one side and then to the other.

Figure 55. Bending wire to a sharp corner for a spring edge.

½" Pipe 8' long

Figure 56. Curving wire for a spring edge.

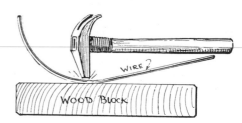

Figure 57. Tying springs to a wire edge.

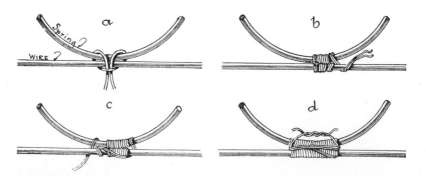

Finally, wrap the twine around the interlacing several times to bind all tightly together, and tie it (Figure 57).

For production work, clips can be obtained to fasten edge wire to springs (Figure 58). Special pliers are made for this purpose (Figure 59).

Figure 58. Edge-wire fastened to spring with a clip.

Figure 59. Spring clip pliers for 5-prong clips.

Questions

1. In making a spring edge, why should the wire be bent to the proper shape before attaching it to the springs?
2. How is wire bent to a desired edge?
3. How is the wire fastened to the spring edge?

TYING SPRINGS CROSSWISE

When the springs have been tied to the desired height, the next step is to tie them crosswise. Care must be taken not to draw the cross twines so tight as to pull down the springs, since this would loosen the pieces of twine already tied in the other direction. However, they must be drawn and tied in order to prevent the springs from moving or tipping to the sides.

Tools and Equipment

Hammer; shears

Materials

Spring twine; tacks

43

Procedure

1. *Measuring Spring Twine.*
   For round or stuffed seats in chairs or stools, hold the twine over the first row of springs, allowing about 2 inches to each spring for knots.

   For flat seats, especially where loose cushions are used, allow enough twine to make a return tie at each end. The return tie must be long enough to go over the top of the first spring, and be tied to the top of the second spring.

2. *Cutting Spring Twine.*
   Cut as many pieces of twine as there are rows of springs, so that all the pieces of twine will be of equal length, and all may be tacked on one end before tying the springs.

3. *Fastening Spring Twine to the Frame.*
   - Place two slip tacks, ½ inch apart, in line with each row of springs. This is especially necessary where there is a strain in pulling down the springs.
   - For round or stuffed seats, where no return twine is necessary, fasten the end of each twine around the two tacks, and drive the tacks down (Figure 60).

Figure 60. Crosstying between springs.

   - On flat seats where a return twine is used, fasten the twine around the two tacks at the proper place to allow for the return twine, and drive the tacks down. This provides two lengths of twine to work with at each row of springs—the first or long twine, and the short return twine.

44

4. *Tying Springs Crosswise—Round Seats.*
- On round or stuffed seats, knot the twine to both top coils of each spring.
- Loop the twine around one of the tacks, pull down to the desired height, and drive this tack down. Loop the twine around the second tack, and drive this tack down.
- Proceed the same with each row until all rows of springs have been tied down to the desired height.

5. *Tying Springs Crosswise—Flat Seats.*
- For flat seats, especially where loose cushions are used, loop the first or long twine around the top coils of each spring, omitting the outer coil at each end.
- Loop the twine around one of the tacks, pull down to the desired height, and drive this tack down. Loop the twine around the second tack, and drive this tack down. This looping of the first twine permits each spring to be moved in a straight line after it has been pulled down to the desired height.
- Follow with the return twine from each end, draw the outer coil down even with the middle spring, knot the return twine over each loop, and finally fasten it to the middle spring. The knotting of the return twine over each loop will now hold the spring in its permanent position.

Questions
1. Why are springs tied crosswise?
2. What will be the result if cross twines are drawn too tight?

CROSSTYING SPRINGS

Crossties add stability and prevent the burlap from sagging into the open spaces between the springs.

For a firmer and more durable job, the so-called eight-way tie is used (Figure 61). This method has eight knots of twine tied to each spring. Care must be taken not to draw the twine so tight as to pull down the springs, since this would loosen the twine already tied in another direction.

Tools and Equipment
Hammer; shears

Figure 61. Eight-way crosstie on springs.

Materials

Spring twine; tacks

Procedure

1. *Placing Tacks.*
   Place a slip tack at each corner and between each row of springs.

2. *Measuring Spring Twine.*
   Hold the twine over a diagonal row of springs, allowing about 2 inches to each spring for knots.

3. *Cutting Twines.*
   Cut as many pieces of twine as needed, so that all the twines may be tacked at one end before tying.

4. *Crosstying Springs.*
   • Fasten the ends of the twines to tacks in the back and on one side, and drive the tacks down.
   • Knot the twine to each spring and at each intersection of twines (Figure 61).
   • Fasten the twines to the tacks in the front and on the remaining side, and drive the tacks down.

Questions

1. Why are springs crosstied?
2. What will be the result if cross twines are drawn too tight?

46

NONSAGGING SPRINGS

When using nonsagging springs, it is not necessary to tack and stretch webbing as a base, since this spring is fastened directly to the top of the frame (Figure 62).

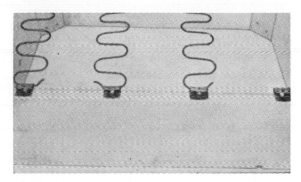

Figure 62. Clips nailed in place for nonsagging springs.

Each spring is fastened to the frame with a special clip. These clips are made in various shapes for the different styles of construction, and are insulated to prevent noises while the furniture is in use (see nonsagging springs, Figure 41).

Tools and Equipment

Hammer

Materials

Nonsagging spring; clips; nails; helicals

Procedure

1. *Measuring for Length of Spring.*
   To determine the length of the nonsagging spring, tack a narrow strip of cardboard to one end of the opening, and then raise the cardboard strip to the height of the spring desired. Measure across the opening with the cardboard, marking the opposite end. Cut the springs to size by measuring each length against the cardboard.

2. *Fastening the Clips to the Frame.*
   • Determine the number of rows of springs for the opening.
   • Nail a clip at the front and back of the frame for each row

47

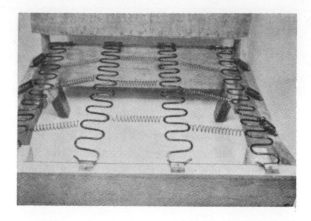

Figure 63. Helical springs set between rows and on the side of the end rows.

of springs. Make certain that the looped end of the clip overhangs the inside edge of the frame by approximately ⅛ inch (Figures 62 and 63). This will permit the spring to swivel freely within the clip, allowing maximum spring action and preventing noise.

3. *Installing the Springs.*
  • Hook the spring end into the clips. It is important to alternate the direction of the bent ends of the spring (Figure 62). If the bent end of the first spring points to the right, the bent end of the next spring should point to the left, and so on throughout the entire installation. This alternating pattern puts the closed loops opposite each other, allowing the links or helical springs to be attached in a straight line.
  • Nail down the upper part of the clip.
  • Place the helical springs between the rows (Figure 63). This will prevent the springs from tipping sideways, and also prevent the burlap from sagging between the rows of springs.

Questions
  1. Why is webbing unnecessary when using this type of spring?
  2. Why are clips insulated?
  3. Why should the looped end of the clip overhang the inside edge of the frame?
  4. Why is it important to alternate the direction of bent ends of the spring?
  5. Why are helical springs used?

48

Procedure 3.   Stuffing

PREPARATION FOR STUFFING

All openings (whether over webbing or springs) must have a piece of burlap to cover the opening, to form a foundation for the stuffing, and to keep the stuffing above the springs.

Burlap

Burlap is a plain cloth, usually woven from jute yarn (see jute plant, Figure 29). Although Calcutta, India, is the world's largest burlap-manufacturing center, large quantities of jute fiber are shipped directly to the United States in a state ready to be woven into burlap and webbing. For upholstery purposes, burlap is used for covering springs, making roll edges and stitched edges, and covering webbing where no springs are used in that part of the furniture. The standard width of burlap is 40 inches. The grades of burlap are determined by the weight per yard. For example: the standard-width burlap, 40 inches, 8 ounces, weighs 8 ounces per yard. The 10-ounce burlap weighs 10 ounces per yard, and so on.

Some upholsterers use various grades of burlap on different parts of furniture, such as on seats, backs, and arms. It is not advisable, however, especially on custom-built upholstery work, to use anything lighter than the 10-ounce grade.

Burlap is shipped from the mills in bales of 20 bolts, with

Figure 64. Burlap piece 40 inches wide and 100 yards long.

each bolt containing 100 yards (Figure 64). Burlap may also be purchased by the yard in various department stores and at upholstery dealers.

ATTACHING BURLAP

Although it may be a simple procedure to tack a piece of burlap over springs, care must be taken not to pull the burlap so tight as to depress the springs. This would put all the strain on the burlap, which would soon tear away.

Tools and Equipment
Hammer; shears

Materials
Burlap; tacks

Procedure

1. *Measuring for Burlap.*
Measure the size of the opening, or measure over the springs at the widest point.

2. *Cutting the Burlap.*
Cut a piece of burlap large enough to cover the entire opening, reaching over the springs and down to the frame, allowing ¾ inch for overlapping on each edge.

3. *Centering Frame and Burlap.*
Mark the middle of the frame and the piece of burlap in front and back. This will permit getting the burlap on straight and having the same amount on both sides.

4. *Tacking the Burlap.*
• Overlap ¾ inch of burlap, and tack it securely to the back rail, getting the middle of the edge on the middle of the frame.

- Pull the burlap tight enough without depressing the edges of the springs.
- Overlap the burlap in front and tack it to the frame, getting the middle of the burlap edge on the middle of the frame.
- Overlap the burlap on the sides, and tack it to the sides of the frame.

Questions

1. What fabric is generally placed over springs?
2. Why is it so important not to pull this fabric so tight that the spring is depressed?
3. How much allowance should be made for overlap?
4. Why should the burlap and the frame be centered in front and back?

ROLL EDGE ON WOOD

A roll edge is necessary to keep the stuffing on the edge of the wood. Without it, the stuffing would soon work away from the edge, allowing the bare wood to wear out the covering and spoil the shape of the upholstering.

Tools and Equipment

Hammer; shears

Materials

Burlap; tacks; stuffing

Figure 65. Roll edge on side of chair seat.

Figure 66. Roll edge on straight wood.

Procedure

1. *Making a Roll Edge on Straight Wood.*
   - Blind-tack a strip of burlap on the outer edge of the wood. The width of the burlap depends on the size roll wanted. It will be of great assistance in forming the roll, if the burlap has been turned straight with the threads, so that the lateral threads may serve as a guide in forming the roll.
   - Fill the burlap with stuffing, the amount of which depends upon the size roll wanted.
   - Twist the burlap upward into the roll and tack the burlap on top (Figure 66).

   For production work, a roll edge may be purchased by the yard. With this type of roll edge, it is necessary only to tack the manufactured roll edge to the frame, making certain that the overhang of the roll is equally distributed over the edge of the frame (Figure 68).

Figure 67. Commercial roll edge ready to be tacked on.

Figure 68. Tacking a manufactured roll edge to the frame.

52

2. *Making a Roll Edge on Curved Wood.*

- Blind-tack a pleated strip of burlap on the outer edge of the wood (Figure 69.) The number and size of the pleats will depend upon the size roll wanted. The pleated burlap will permit the roll edge to extend out over the frame on a curve.
- Fill the burlap with stuffing, the amount depending upon the size roll wanted (Figure 70).
- Twist the burlap into the roll and tack it on top.

Figure 69. Tacking burlap to a round arm for a roll edge.

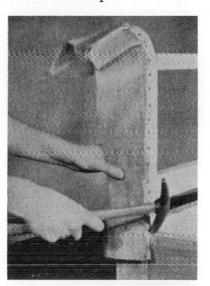

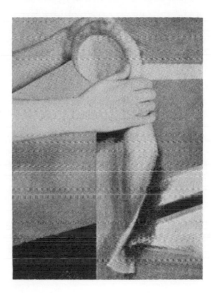

Figure 70. Stuffing the roll edge on a round arm.

Figure 71. Completed roll edge.

Questions

1. Why is a roll edge put on wood?
2. What will determine the amount of stuffing to be used in making a roll edge?
3. What will determine the width of burlap for a roll edge?
4. In making a roll edge on curved wood or around a corner, why must pleats be laid in the burlap while blind-tacking?

STITCHED EDGE

Forming the stitched edge is as important to the appearance and durability of a piece of furniture as is the proper placing and tying of the springs. When the stitched edge has been formed, the piece is ready for stuffing; that is to say, it has been molded into shape, and the desired outlines have been formed.

Tools and Equipment

Straight and curved needles; shears; regulator; hammer

Materials

Burlap; stuffing; stitching twine; tacks

Procedure

1. *Sewing Burlap to Make a Stitched Edge.*
   Sew a strip of burlap, about 4 inches from the front edge, to the burlap over the springs. The width of the burlap will depend upon the size of edge wanted. Sew the burlap straight with the threads, so that the lateral threads of the burlap may serve as a guide in forming the edge.

2. *Stuffing the Edge.*
   Fill the burlap with stuffing, the amount of which depends upon the size edge wanted (Figure 72).

3. *Fastening the Burlap to Front.*
   Sew the burlap to the wire (Figure 73).

4. *Forming and Stitching the Edge.*
   • Regulate the stuffing forward.
   • First-row stitch with a straight needle, drawing the stuffing forward (Figure 74).

54

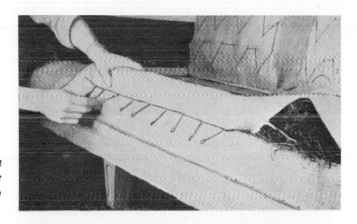

Figure 72. Stuffing a stitched edge on a wire edge. Burlap is pinned to the wire front.

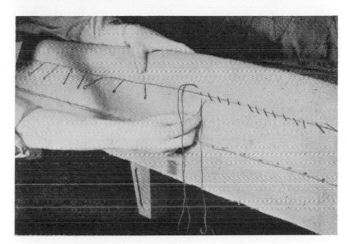

Figure 73. Sewing the burlap to the wire front. The pins are removed as the sewing progresses.

Figure 74. Stitching the first row with a straight needle, drawing the stuffing forward.

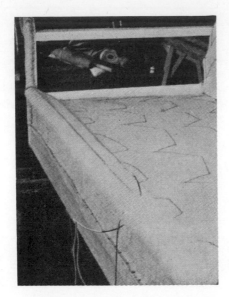

Figure 75. Stitching the second row with a curved needle, forming the roll in the edge.

- Second-row stitch with a curved needle, forming a roll (Figure 75).
- Third-row stitch with a curved needle, forming a smaller roll.
- More rows of stitches may be added where a high and sharp edge is wanted. The more rows of stitches used, the firmer the edge.
- For production work, a stitched edge, ready for attaching can be purchased by the yard (Figure 76). This type of stitched edge is firmly stuffed and sewn, ready for attaching, and, when properly attached, will hold up far better than the hand-made edge.

5. Attaching the Ready-Made Stitched Edge.
- Sew the inner border of the stitched edge firmly to the burlap about 3 inches from the front wire (depending upon the overhang desired) making certain that the overhang of the edge is the same all across the front.
- Sew the front part of the edge firmly to the front wire edge (Figure 76).

Questions
1. What is the difference between a roll edge and a stitched edge?
2. Why should burlap be sewn straight with the threads?
3. What will determine the amount of stuffing in a stitched edge?
4. What will determine the width of burlap for a stitched edge?
5. What is necessary where a high and sharp edge is needed?

Figure 76. Attaching a ready-made stitched edge.

STUFFING

The preceding sections have explained the procedures preparatory to the actual stuffing process: attaching burlap, making a roll edge, and making a stitched edge. When the preliminary steps are completed, the piece of furniture is ready to be stuffed. Stuffing materials are plentiful and varied. In the following section, some of these materials are discussed and the stuffing procedure is explained.

Kapok (Silk Floss)

Kapok (silk floss) is the silky fiber which adheres to the seeds in the seed pods of a tree known as *ceiba pentandra*. This large tree grows best in Java, which has the proper soil and climatic conditions. These pods are 4 to 5 inches long. When the seeds are gathered, the floss is removed and tightly compressed by machinery. A bale of kapok, which scarcely measures 2 by 2 by 2 feet may contain as much as 200 pounds. This excessive compression, however, removes from the floss all the qualities which a good upholstery filling should possess (Figure 77).

When the bales are opened, the kapok must be adapted for upholstery in a machine called a picking box, the huge wooden arms of which revolve on a steel axis at a speed of from 500 to 750 r.p.m. The floss emerges quite fluffy, springy, and lifelike.

Then, too, the kapok, as it comes in the bale, is mixed with considerable foreign matter, such as seeds, sand, and particles of pods. These foreign particles, being heavier than the floss, twirl

57

Figure 77. Kapok as imported in bales.

around the outside of the axis in the picking machine and are caught on a tray attached to the bottom of the machine.

When put through the machine once, the kapok is called first-run or single-process kapok. When it is put through the machine a second time, its filling qualities for upholstery are increased about 25 percent; it is then called superfine kapok.

The kapok fiber is very silky, and does not absorb moisture. It is used extensively for camp mattresses, boat cushions, and life preservers, in addition to making toss pillows for furniture.

Moss

Southern moss is known also as Louisiana moss and Spanish moss. The latter name is misleading because the moss does not actually grow in Spain. It is found along the coast from Texas to Florida northward to Virginia and southward to southern Brazil. However, Louisiana and Florida are the only places where it is abundant enough to be picked commercially. The Florida moss, which is very short, makes a very poor upholstery filler and is not used much.

This moss is not a parasite, as is commonly supposed; the trees furnish its lodging, but it derives its sustenance from the air. The seeds, like those of the dandelion or buttercup, have a parachute attached which carries them through the air, and they grow on whatever tree they adhere to. Plants usually absorb moisture from the soil through the roots; this moss, however, absorbs moisture from the air through tiny scales that cover every part of its stem and leaves.

Figure 78. Southern moss hanging from trees.

Moss is gathered throughout the year. It is picked from the ground after being blown from the trees; it is collected from felled trees, and pulled from living trees. The moss is most abundant in marsh and swamp land (Figure 78).

As the moss comes from the trees, there is a green coating around the fiber, which must be removed before the fiber can be used for stuffing. The process of removing this coating is called "curing" or "rotting." The fresh moss is put in piles about 5 feet high and is thoroughly soaked. In about ten days, the piles begin to get hot and the outer covering begins to rot. In about six weeks, much of the bark has disappeared, leaving the inner hairlike strand, which becomes darker and darker as the process continues. In about twelve weeks only the black fiber remains. The green moss, after being cured for about ninety days, yields only about a 20 percent return of black fiber. After the curing is complete, the fiber must be thoroughly dried. In the moss-producing regions, it is quite common to see rocks, sheds, and clotheslines covered with moss exposed to the sun and wind.

The dry moss must be ginned. The ginning is a picking and combing process which opens up the fibers and removes sticks, dirt, burrs, and so on. To produce good clean moss, the ginning must be repeated four times in most cases. Moss is graded as XX moss, XXX moss, and XXXX moss. That means that XXX moss is not cured as long as the XXXX moss, having, therefore, a gray color, and that it is only single-ginned, leaving a lot of sticks and burrs adhering to the fiber. The XXXX moss is cured longer and, therefore, has a black color. It is double-ginned, making it a cleaner and better upholstery filler. The grades of moss can be determined by the color. Moss is sold in bales of about 100 pounds.

Curled Hair

The curled hair used as an upholstery filler in this country comes from horse tails and manes imported from South America, where vast herds of semiwild horses roam the ranges, and are rounded up and clipped about once a year by natives who follow this occupation as a means of livelihood. Cattle hair and hog hair are also used.

Before it is ready to be used for upholstery, the raw hair must go through a number of processes:

1. *Sorting.*
   The hair is sorted into various colors, lengths, and textures as follows:
   • Horse-tail hair is the longest and hardest and most valuable.
   • Cattle-hair, long but soft, is next in quality and value.
   • Mane hair is the softest but also the shortest.
   • Hog hair, which is taken from the hogs killed at the packing plants, is not sorted according to color; it is all classified as gray. Being short but hard, it is ranked fourth in value. Since hog hair cannot be spun or curled alone, it must be mixed with horse or cattle hair.

2. *Sterilizing.*
   The hair is washed in a solution of acetic acid to deodorize and clean it thoroughly. The washed hair is then dried on a revolving platform by electric fans. When it has been thoroughly dried, it is ready to be spun into rope form.

3. *Spinning.*
   The loose hair is twisted very tightly into ropes from 30 to 40 feet long and about ½ to ¾ inch thick. Great care is exercised to insure the curling of every hair in the mixture. Then the ends

of these 40 foot ropes are joined together and plaited into 20 foot strands. This method safeguards the long fillers against breakage.

4. Curling.

In rope form, the twisted hair is resterilized in large vats of boiling, chemically treated water, for about 2 hours, at a temperature of 212 degrees F. This gives the hair a truly "permanent wave" and each individual hair is curled into a miniature spring.

5. Drying.

From the boiling vats, the ropes are taken to the drying room, where they are kept from 8 to 10 hours at a temperature of 150 degrees F. (Figure 79).

6. Seasoning.

To destroy completely any animal or dye odors, the ropes are placed in an airing room or glass shed, like a greenhouse, where they are given a sun bath for several days. Then they are put into a seasoning vault for about 90 days until they are ready for carding.

7. Carding.

The ropes are unraveled in the reverse direction from that in which they were spun. This is done by hand with the aid of revolving hooks. They are then put into the carding machine which pulls them apart or combs them leaving the hair in a fluffy resilient mass. As a safeguard against breakage, the long curled hair is usually packed into loosely filled bags of about 50 pounds each.

Figure 79. Curled hair drying in rope form.

61

Figure 80. Rubberized hair, cut to fit the back of a chair.

Rubberized Hair

Rubberized hair is made by impregnating curled hair with pure rubber without injury to the hair and without leaving the finished material sticky or tacky. Rubberized hair can be used anywhere in upholstered furniture—in arms, backs, and seats, customarily in combination with springs and cotton felt. It can be cut to conform to any requirements, and may be tacked or sewn into place (Figure 80).

Rubberized hair is extremely light in weight; and because it is composed of a vast number of tightly curled animal hairs bonded together with rubber, it is self-ventilating and resilient. It is sold ready to use. For production work, rubberized hair is available in cut-to-size pieces and shapes for all types of furniture and also, in sheets 24 by 72 inches and in 25 yard rolls in widths of 18, 24, 36, and 48 inches. It comes in various thicknesses from ¾ to 3 inches which may be laminated together to form the desired shape (Figure 81).

Rubberized hair is also made in various densities. The soft density is used over arms and in backs of furniture, where maximum amount of set resistance is not necessary. The medium density is used in arms, backs, and seats of furniture, where average set resistance must be combined with reasonable serviceability. The firm density is used in all applications where maximum life, resiliency, and resistance to setting are important. When in doubt, use the firmer density.

Figure 81. A tapered bolster with sheets of rubberized hair laminated together for size and shape.

To prevent the hair from coming through the covering, it is necessary to place a layer or more of cotton felt over the rubberized hair.

STUFFING WITH MUSLIN COVER

For upholstery work, unbleached muslin is used as a first covering over the stuffing, especially when the upholstery coverings are to be cut to various shapes and sizes to fit on the seats, backs, and arms of the furniture. Also, the use of muslin permits pulling the stuffing to its desired shape and firmness before putting on the covering.

Unbleached muslin may be purchased in most department stores, and comes in 36 and 39 inch widths.

The use of muslin for a first covering is also desirable when the top cover is to be of silk, satin, or damask. The stuffing can be drawn down to the desired shape and firmness while attaching the muslin cover, thereby preventing strain on the top cover.

When stuffing furniture, three items must be given careful attention: (1) The stuffing must be picked through to remove all lumps. (2) It must be spread evenly to avoid holes or lumps when the work has been completed. (3) It must be sewed down securely to prevent shifting.

Tools and Equipment

Hammer; shears; straight and curved needles

Materials

Stuffing; stitching twine; tacks; muslin

Procedure

1. *Place Stuffing for Sewing.*
   - Pick over the stuffing, removing all lumps.
   - Place about three-fourths of the total amount of stuffing evenly. The rest will be used to level off the top after the sewing is done.

2. *Sew Stuffing Down.*
   Sew the stuffing down to the burlap, which serves as a foundation or bottom.

3. *Place Top Stuffing.*
   - Distribute the remainder of the stuffing evenly over the top of the stuffing that has been sewed down.
   - Draw over the muslin cover to the shape and firmness desired. To avoid wrinkles, start tacking the muslin at the middle of each edge, working a little at a time to each corner or end.

Questions

1. What is the first step in stuffing?
2. Why must stuffing be sewed down?
3. Why is not *all* the stuffing sewed down?

Procedure 4.   Covering

Selection of Coverings

Covering materials for upholstering should be selected only after careful, serious consideration. For example, when a chair will receive much use, the covering should have good wearing qualities and soft colors. On the other hand, a piece of furniture that will be used less frequently may have a covering with a finer texture and brighter colors.

After the quality and color of covering are determined, the next important step is to decide whether the fabric should be plain, patterned, or striped. While plain or subdued patterns of upholstery coverings are most frequently chosen for upholstering modern pieces of furniture, there are certain pieces of furniture on which a figured or striped fabric would be more suitable. The choice, of course, depends on how the room is decorated, what style or period the furniture is, and how frequently the piece will be used.

Striped Material

When selecting a wide-striped material for covering, allowance must be made for waste, since the stripes on the seat covering must match those stripes on the inside and outside back, as well as the stripes on the front seat borders (Figure 82). The welt for narrow-striped material must all be cut either crosswise or on a bias. See page 89. On wide-striped material, one of the stripes in the material may be selected for welt.

65

Figure 82. A chair covered with striped materials. All welt is cut crosswise. Note matching stripes in the seat, front border, and front welt.

Figure 83. Love seat with floral design and contrasting welt.

Large Pattern or Motif

Since coverings that have a large pattern or motif must be centered on each cushion top, inside, and outside back, careful planning is necessary before purchasing or cutting the material. Do not buy a covering which has such a large pattern that the design will have to be cut off to fit the furniture.

With patterned covers, welt is frequently made from a piece of plain material, such as sateen or denim. The color of this material should be selected to match one of the colors in the patterned material (Figure 83).

Fabrics

Fabrics are very important to the upholsterer because the most visible feature of the finished product is the cover. It is, therefore, essential that you have a good basic understanding of fabrics in order to make covers and to talk intelligently about cover selections.

Although customers rarely ask for the fiber content or the type of weave in a fabric, a knowledge of such background information not only gives the upholsterer a feeling of confidence, but also provides answers to the more practical questions that may be asked.

The so-called soft coverings which may be made of cotton, silk, rayon, or a combination of several materials are too numerous to describe in detail here. Nevertheless, some other materials, the source, qualities, and use of which may be less familiar are discussed.

Denim

Denim is a strong, twilled cotton fabric with superior wearing qualities which is woven of single yarn, both in warp and filling. It is made frequently with a mottled surface, that is, dark blue, gray, or brown with flecks of white. It also comes in plain colors, or with a small pattern woven into it.

While heavy denim is used for men's overalls and working clothes, the lighter denims are used for upholstery work on seats of furniture which contain loose cushions. Covers are often made of "pull denim," while figured denim is used for upholstering furniture, especially Bahama lounges (Figure 217).

Figure 84. Plastic covered furniture in a waiting room.

Figure 85. Plastic covering on furniture in a showroom.

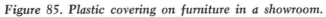

Figure 86. Floral pattern of plastic with appearance of fabric.

Figure 87. Imitation embossed leather.

Plastic (Vinyl) Covering

Plastic covers are used extensively on furniture in waiting rooms (Figure 84), showrooms (Figure 85), and numerous other places. Whether the furniture is made of wrought iron, tubular steel, rattan or a wood base, plastic material with its intricate patterns and vast variety of colors is very appropriate as a cover.

Vinyl plastics, called by various trade names like Naugahyde, are synthetic resins derived from limestone, coal, and salt. The plastic is a white powder resembling corn starch or flour, and, when properly compounded, it has many of the characteristics of rubber.

The powder is mixed with stabilizers, plasticizers, color pigments, and other ingredients to produce specific qualities. In a process called "calendering," this group of raw materials is thoroughly mixed in a machine and then further blended under high heat and pressure, which softens the ingredients into a doughlike mass. The surface of the calendered material is then printed, embossed, two-toned, or left as a plain color.

Plastic can be obtained with a strong fabric backing that provides strength and durability for long-lasting, trouble-free service. This fabric backing is not a surface coating, but is mechanically fused into the fabric for permanent adhesion. The

69

Figure 88. *Imitation calfskin.*

advantage of upholstering with this type of covering is the ease with which it can be applied since the backing is a knitted fabric that can be stretched eight ways. Round and oval pieces can be put on as easily as the square pieces.

While plastic is a tough material resistant to abrasion, it is also soft and pliable enough to be neatly tailored. Since it contains nothing that will dry out and is not affected by cold, heat, sun, oil or grease, plastic will not crack or split or deteriorate with age.

Another attractive feature of plastic material is its easy care. Soil is removed and the plastic is restored by washing with a mild soap and warm water and polishing with a dry cloth. An occasional damp-cloth wiping will keep the colors fresh and new looking.

Plastic is not only practical, but decorative as well. A large number of appropriate patterns may be had for various types and styles of furniture (Figures 86, 87 & 88), and the vast selection of colors available makes it possible to harmonize with any color scheme in the room.

Some of these textures reproduce exactly the look of fine linen (Figure 86), fragile grass cloth, straw woven rush, antiqued leather (Figure 87), and other natural products (Figure 88).

The smaller intricate patterns (Figure 86) are appropriate on such pieces as headboards (Figure 212), dinette chairs, and card tables. On the other hand, the larger patterns are usually used on larger pieces of furniture such as overstuffed chairs (Figure 88).

Plastic is sold by the yard and is usually 54 inches wide. It comes in rolls approximately 30 yards long.

Custom Quilted Fabric

Quilted fabric is another type of attractive furniture covering. Not too many years ago, ladies turned their sewing lessons into social events called quilting bees where they worked together to produce exquisite needlework and quilting.

Today materials can be sent to modern factories to be made into quilted bedspreads or upholstery in a variety of quilting patterns (Figures 89 & 90). The fabric is either quilted on plain material or on patterned material.

Interesting combinations of plain and quilted material can be utilized when upholstering various types of furniture. On some pieces, only the inside backs and cushion tops are covered with the quilted fabric. The remaining areas of the piece are then covered with the same material in an unquilted state (Figure 91).

Figure 89. Quilted pattern (mystic maze) on plain material.

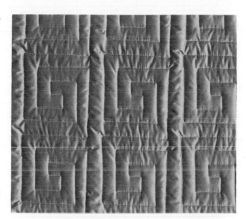

Figure 90. Quilted material made into a bedspread.

Figure 91. Sofa covered with quilted material on inside back and on cushion tops only. The balance is covered with the same material unquilted.

Cambric

Cambric is a cotton cloth which is made dustproof by sizing or glazing and is available in black or white. The white cambric is used for pillow casings which are to be stuffed with kapok. The black cambric is used for tacking underneath the furniture since the black color is inconspicuous and the dustproofing prevents the dust in the stuffing from falling to the floor. Cambric is 24 to 36 inches wide and may be purchased in most department stores.

Scotchgard

Scotchgard is the registered trade name for a family of fluoro-chemicals developed to protect fabrics and leather from stains and soil. The finish resists both oil and water thereby preventing both oil and water based stains from penetrating the treated fabric. Staining material will "sit" on the treated fabric surface until it is blotted away or shaken off. Once applied, Scotchgard protectors cannot be seen, felt or smelled, and will not alter the color or the strength of the treated material.

Scotchgard protector in spray-can form can be applied at home in do-it-yourself fashion or by authorized applicators at the mill or tannery. The aerosol cans are available throughout the country in hardware and department stores and in some cases, in upholstery shops. Many upholstery shops treat all repaired or new upholstery covers with Scotchgard as an added service.

Scotchgard will set at room temperature and will repel oily and watery stains after a 30 minute drying period.

MEASURING COVERING FOR SIZE

Always measure the widest and longest part of each piece of covering required; and, since very few coverings are made that can be cut or put on in either direction, it is very important that the coverings are all cut in the proper direction. Each piece of cover should be measured and the length and width should be marked.

When measuring cushion tops for the size of the covering, especially where the cushions are wider in front than in the rear, it is important to measure the front edge of the cushion for width. Do not measure through the center of the cushion. It is good policy always to measure each piece of covering width × length, regardless of size. For example, the seat cushion measures 22 inches wide and 20 inches deep, while the back cushion measures 20 inches wide and 22 inches high. While the sizes given are exactly the same, the coverings must be cut in the proper direction. The sizes for the given example would then be listed as: seat cushion 22 to 20 inches and the back cushion 20 by 22 inches.

PLANNING AND CUTTING COVERS

Cutting the furniture covering is an important step in upholstery. The fabrics used are, as a rule, expensive, and to use 5 yards of material when, by skillful planning and cutting, 4½ yards would suffice, makes a considerable difference in the cost.

When cutting covers, especially those with large designs and motifs, it is best to cut the large pieces first (seat, back, outside back, arms) as these may require centering of a pattern. The smaller pieces should, if possible, be cut from the waste.

Determine first the width of the material and then all sizes wanted; thus, all the pieces may be marked out before cutting. In measuring covers, always measure the width first to insure cutting the correct way. Covers that have a pattern or that brush with a nap cannot be cut crosswise.

Tools and Equipment

Shears; yardstick; patterns; chalk

Materials

Covering; muslin or denim

Procedure

1. *Placing Patterned Material.*
   - The pattern in the material must come in the center of the seat or back (Figure 83).
   - When the pattern is a medallion or floral bouquet, or any other form or motif having a definite top and bottom, the pattern must run toward the back on seats, and toward the top on backs and arms.
   - Pile fabrics, such as velour, mohair, velvet, etc., must be put on so that the nap brushes forward on seats and downward on backs and arms.

2. *Mark Around Pattern.*

3. *Cut Over as Outlined.*
   Where certain portions of seats, backs, and arms meet, covers should be cut only large enough for that which is exposed. Piece out the remainder with cheaper material under arms and back. Muslin or denim are commonly used for this purpose (Figures 92 & 93).

   This is a handy way to save both money and material. It is a good idea to keep it in mind when selecting and buying upholstery fabric in order to purchase the correct amount.

Questions

1. In cutting covering, why should large pieces be cut first?
2. How should material having a medallion or floral design be cut?

Figure 92. Pull denim sewn to the rear of the seat cover.

Figure 93. Pull denim sewn to the bottom of the back cover.

3. How should pile fabrics such as velour, mohair, etc., be cut?
4. Why should width always be measured first?
5. Why should covering be pieced with cheaper material where certain parts of seats, backs, and arms meet?

MACHINE-SEWING UPHOLSTERY COVERS

Most home sewing machines will sew through even heavy upholstery coverings. However, when sewing over cross seams, it is best to turn the wheel of the sewing machine slowly by hand, in order to prevent breaking or bending sewing-machine needles.

Since the proper sewing of coverings affects endurance as well as appearance, the following important rules must be kept in mind.

1. In making seams, the stitching should be at least ½ inch from the edge of the goods, so that the strain on the cover will not cause the seams to open.

2. For heavier coverings, set the stitches on the sewing machine on *Large*, and use a heavy-duty thread.

3. The top and bottom pieces of covering must be held firmly so that they will not gather under the machine during the sewing operation.

Tools and Equipment
    Sewing machine and accessories; shears

Materials
    Covering; thread; cord (where welt is to be used)

Procedure

1. *Sewing Plain Material.*
    • Where stitching shows on plain material, the color of the thread must match the color of the covering.
    • Seams must be properly sewed and thoroughly pressed so that they will be as inconspicuous as possible.

2. *Sewing Patterned Material.*
    The pattern must match perfectly or the seam will be conspicuous because of the broken pattern.

3. *Sewing Welt.*
    See page 89, Welting.

Questions

1. In sewing covering, how much material should be allowed for seams? Why?
2. What grade of covering requires a large stitch?
3. How can gathering of material be prevented?
4. What color thread should be used in sewing plain material?
5. When sewing patterned material, why must the pattern at the seams be perfectly matched?

PUTTING ON COVERS

When covering furniture be sure to center the floral design or motif, to get the cover on straight, and to make the pleats both definite and neat.

Tools and Equipment
    Hammer; shears; curved needle

Materials
    Cover; stitching twine; tacks

Procedure

1. *Centering the Cover with the Frame.*
   - Mark the middle of the front and back of the frame.
   - Mark the middle of the cover in the front and back. These marks will help to get the cover on straight, with the same amount of material on each side.

2. *Slip-tacking the Cover.*
   - Slip-tack the cover to the frame in back, centering the cover on the frame.
   - Slip-tack the cover in front, drawing the cover to the firmness desired.
   - Slip-tack the cover on the sides.
   - Make sure that the cover is properly centered and that the lines of the pattern are straight; then begin tacking at the middle of the front, back, and sides, releasing the slip tacks one at a time, and adjusting the material to the desired firmness without wrinkles as the tacks are driven in. To avoid wrinkles, begin tacking in the middle of the back, front, and sides, and work toward the corners.

3. *Making the Square-Corner Pleat.*
   Laying and making pleats on the corners of the covering should be done as neatly and carefully as was the upholstery. On seats, the front corner pleats should always lay toward the rear, while on backs and arms, the pleats should lay downward. The smaller pleats can usually be drawn firm enough to lay snugly, while the larger pleats (Figures 95 & 97) should be pinned or tacked down, and then sewn shut with a curved needle and twine.

4. *Laying Pleats for Square Corners.*
   - Draw the cover down to the desired firmness on the front and sides. Tack in front up to about 2 inches from the corner.
   - Tack the side cover to the front near the corner.
   - Cut away the surplus goods under the pleat (Figure 94).
   - Fold the goods in front, and lay the pleat to the rear.
   - Temporarily pin or tack the pleat directly on the corner (Figure 95).
   - Sew the pleat shut with a curved needle and twine.

5. *Laying Pleats for Rounded Corners—V Pleat.*
   - Draw the cover down to the desired firmness and tack it

77

Figure 94. Trimming off the excess covering under the pleat.

Figure 95. Pleat temporarily tacked and ready for sewing.

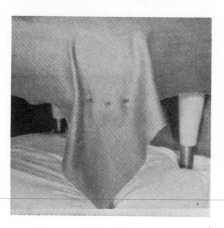

Figure 96. Covering drawn down with surplus on each side.

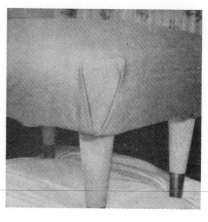

Figure 97. Large V pleat ready to be sewn.

directly on the corner, leaving the same amount of surplus cover on both the side and the front (Figure 96).

• Fold the pleats facing each other to form a V (Figure 97).

Questions

1. What three items must be considered when putting on covers?
2. What is the meaning of slip tack?
3. How are wrinkles avoided in covering?
4. How should pleats be laid on corners?

BLIND-TACKING OUTSIDE COVERINGS

On outside backs and on outside arms which are straight across the top, the cover may be blind-tacked. Blind-tacking means tacking the top edge of the outside piece of covering on the top, with the wrong side of the covering to the outside.

Tools and Equipment

Hammer; shears; curved needle

Supplies

Cardboard; tacks; twine

Procedure

Blind-Tacking the Covering.
- Center the outside piece of covering on the frame. This will assure having the same amount of covering on each side.
- Tack the cover to the top edge. The tacks should be about 6 inches apart.
- Tack a strip of heavy cardboard over the tacks. This will make a straight joint after the cover is drawn over (Figure 98).
- Draw the cover over the cardboard.
- Tack the bottom of the cover to the bottom of the frame.
- Fold the sides of the cover under.
- Baste the folded sides of the cover with large tacks or pins.
- Sew the sides of the cover to the sides of the frame (Figure 99).

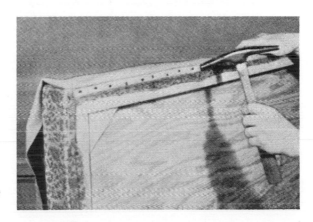

Figure 98. Blind-tacking the outside back covering.

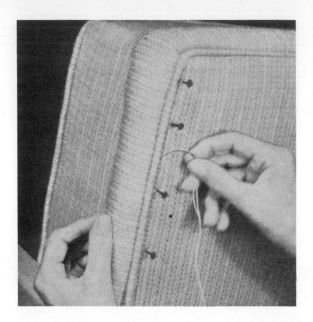

Figure 99. Sewing the sides of the outside piece of covering to the sides of the frame.

Questions

1. Why should the outside cover be centered with the frame?
2. Why is a piece of cardboard used in blind-tacking?

ROUND-ARM UPHOLSTERY

A great number of upholstered pieces of furniture are of the round-arm and round-back variety. The larger round arms and round backs usually are finished with a covered wood panel (Figure 100).

Tools and Equipment

Shears; curved needle; hammer

Materials

Cover; twine; tacks

Procedure

1. *Placing the Cover.*
Draw the cover down to the firmness desired.

80

Figure 100. Davenport with covered wood panels.

2. Finishing the Front for a Covered Wood Panel.

- Trim the surplus material from the front arm, leaving enough material, however, so that its edge will be covered with the panel.
- Sew a draw twine through the covering ½ inch from the edge (Figure 101).

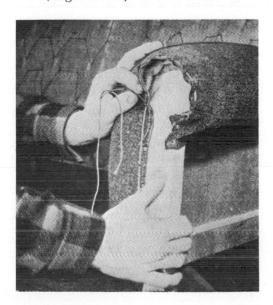

Figure 101. Sewing the draw twine through the covering.

Figure 102. Draw twine pulled firmly and tucked to the arm.

- Draw the twine firmly, each stitch in the twine forming a pleat (Figure 102).
- Tack the ends of the twine down firmly. To prevent the arm covering from coming loose in the event that the twine should tear, it is best to drive a few tacks through the covering between each pleat.

After the outside arm has been tacked down, the covered panel is tacked in place (Figures 105 & 106).

Questions

1. How much cover should be trimmed off the front arm?
2. Why should a few tacks be driven through the covering between the pleats after shirring?

COVERING AND ATTACHING LOOSE WOOD PANELS

A great number of pieces of furniture are upholstered with covered wood panels on each arm. These panels are separate pieces of wood ½ inch thick or they are made of plywood. It is a mystery to most people how the panels are covered and attached to the furniture because no nails are visible.

The panels are covered with the same material as the upholstery covering and are frequently trimmed with a welt covering all around.

Tools and Equipment

   Sewing machine; hammer; shears; regulator

Materials

   Covering; tacks; brads; welt cord; thread

Procedure

1. *Cutting Cover for Panels.*
   - Cut two pieces of covering 1 inch larger than the wood panel.
   - Cut strips of covering (for welt) 1½ inches wide and long enough to reach around both panels.

2. *Covering the Panels.*
   - Lay the panels face down, on the inside of the panel cover.
   - Pull the cover over and tack it to the wood panel (Figure 103).

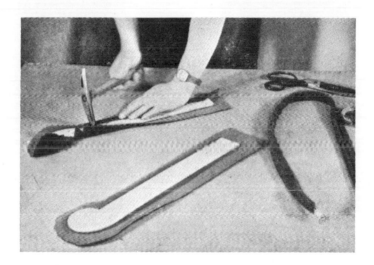

Figure 103. Covering the wood panel.

3. *Making Welt for Panels.*
   - Sew together all 1½ inch strips.
   - Insert a cord and sew it into the welt. See page 89, Welting.

4. *Attaching Welt to Panels.*
   - Tack the welt to the back of the wood panel, letting the covered cord show in front (Figure 104).

83

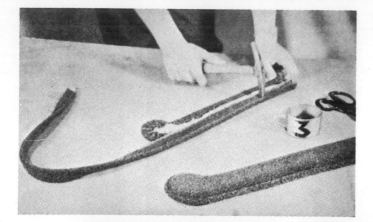

Figure 104. Attaching welt to the wood panel.

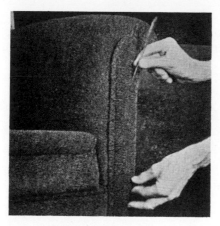

Figure 105. Inserting regulator through cover.

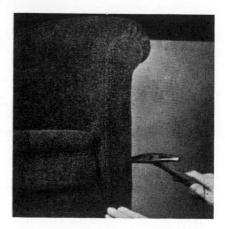

Figure 106. Nailing the panel to the arm.

5. Attaching Covered Panel to Arms.
- Insert a regulator through the cover in the front of the panel, and turn the regulator to form an opening between the threads of the covering.
- Remove the regulator carefully.
- Nail the panel to the arm with small-headed nails (brads).
- Close the threads of the material by scratching over the opening lightly with the regulator.

Questions

1. What is a wood panel?
2. What material is used to cover a wood panel?
3. How should material be cut to cover a wood panel?
4. What is used to trim a wood panel?
5. How are wood-covered panels attached to the arms?

Procedure 5.   Finishing and Trimming

After the piece of furniture has been covered, the finishing touches and trimming must be added. Finishing and trimming materials such as gimp, metaline nails, welting, and fabric skirts are, on the whole, decorative, but they sometimes serve practical functions as well.

The following section describes both the manner in which various trims are made and how they are attached to the furniture to give a neat and professional appearance to the finished piece.

MAKING A LARGE COVERED TACK BUTTON

Procedure

Making a Covered Tack Button.
- Cut a round piece of heavy cardboard or ¼ inch plywood to the size of the button desired.
- Place a large tack or small nail through this cardboard.
- Cut a piece of covering 1½ inches larger than the cardboard.
- Sew a draw twine through the covering all around ½ inch from the edge.
- Place a small layer of cotton felt on the inside of the covering (A, Figure 107). This cotton will give the button a crown and also prevent the cover from being cut by the tack head when the button is nailed in place.
- Place the cardboard, with the tack inserted, over the cotton (B, Figure 107).

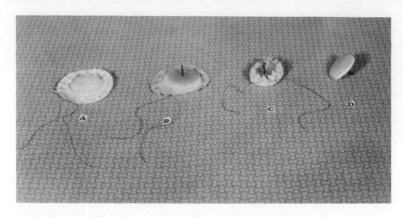

Figure 107. Four steps in making a hand-covered button.

- Draw the twine firmly and tie up the ends (C, Figure 107). The button is now ready to be nailed to the job (D, Figure 107 & Figure 111).

Questions
1. How much larger than the cardboard should the cover be?
2. Why is a piece of cotton felt placed over the tack?

ROUND-ARM UPHOLSTERY WITH A COVERED BUTTON

Round arms as well as rounded backs are frequently finished off with a large covered button (Figure 108).

Tools and Equipment
Shears; curved needle; hammer

Materials
Covers; twine; tacks

Procedure

1. *Placing the Cover.*
Draw the cover down to the firmness desired.

2. *Finishing the Front for a Covered Button.*
   - Trim the surplus material from the front arm leaving enough material so that the edges meet all around (Figure 109).
   - Sew a draw twine through the covering ½ inch from the edge.

Figure 108. Round-arm upholstery with a covered tack button.

Figure 109. Cover trimmed with draw twines shirred.

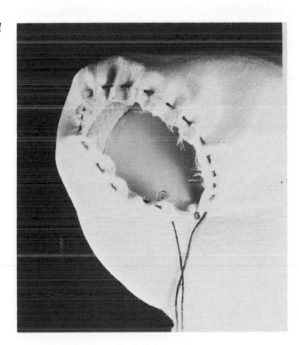

- Draw the twine firmly, forming a pleat at each stitch (Figure 110).
- Tack the ends of the twine down firmly. To prevent the covering from coming loose in the event that the twine should tear, it is best to drive a few tacks through the covering between each pleat (Figure 110).
- The tack button should now be nailed to the job (Figure 111).

Questions

1. How much cover should be trimmed off the front?
2. Why should a few tacks be driven through the covering between the pleats after shirring?

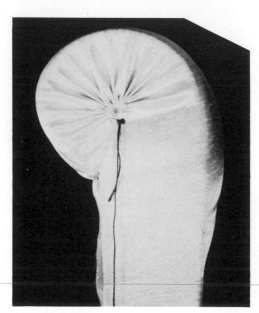

Figure 110. Draw twine pulled firmly and tacked down.

Figure 111. Button nailed to the arm.

WELTING

Welt is a covered cord which is sewn between seams. It is made either from the same fabric as the covering or from plain contrasting colored fabric.

The welt strips are cut 1½ inches wide, and may consist of a number of pieces which are sewn together before inserting the cord.

Tools and Equipment

Sewing machine with equipment; shears

Supplies

Thread; cover; welt cord

Procedure

1. *Cutting Welt Strips.*

The welt strips usually may be cut in any direction of the material since the pattern in the material will not be noticeable in the narrow strip. However, on coverings such as velvet or mohair, it is best to cut *all* welt strips in *one* direction, because the nap on this material would be noticeable if the cutting of the strips is not all in the same direction. Do *not* cut welt strips directly from the roll of material, since, after some of the larger pieces of covering are cut to size and shape, there may be remnants left from which welt strips can be cut (Figure 112).

Figure 112. Cutting strips for well.

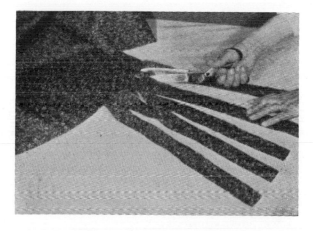

Figure 113. Cutting welt on a bias.

2. *Cutting Welt Strips from Wide-Striped Material.*
When using a wide-striped material for covering, it is best to select *one* of the wide stripes in the material and then cut *all* strips for the welt from this stripe.

3. *Cutting Welt Strips from Narrow-Striped Material.*
On narrow-striped material, the welt strips should all be cut crosswise (Figure 117) or they may be cut on a bias (Figures 113 & 118).

4. *Marking Welt.*
To make welt, it will be necessary to have a welt-foot or zipper-foot attachment for the sewing machine (Figure 115). Although most of the newer model sewing machines come equipped with this type of attachment, it can be purchased in most stores that handle sewing machines.
 • Join all the welt strips together end-to-end.
 • Sew the welt cord into the joined strips (Figure 114). For welt cord, see Figure 25.

5. *Joining Welt Between Seams.*
Sew the covered welt to the right side of the cover ½ inch from the outer edge which is to be joined (Figure 115).

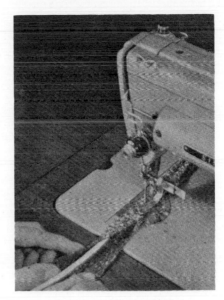

Figure 114. Sewing the welt cord into the joined strips.

6. *Making a Square Corner with Welt.*
   - Make a cut into the welt ½ inch from the edge of the cover where the welt is to turn (Figure 115).
   - Sew directly up to the turn, and with the needle in the covering, turn the welt to a square corner.
   - Sew to the next corner, and repeat on all square corners.

Figure 115. Making a square corner with welt.

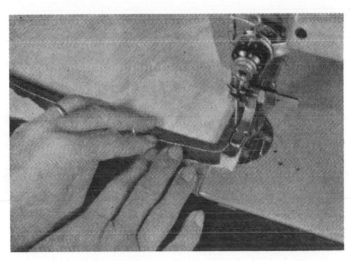

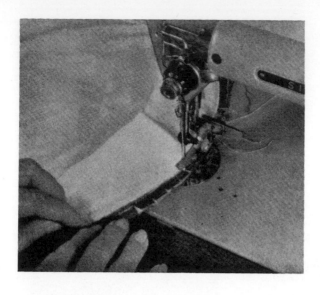

Figure 116. Joining the
top cover to the sewn-
on welt.

7. *Sewing Welt Around Curves.*
   Make a number of cuts into the welt (Figure 116). This will
   prevent the outer edge of the welt from turning upward.

8. *Joining the Cover to the Welt.*
   After the covered welt is sewn to the right side of the covering
   which is to be joined, the other part of the covering is then laid
   face-to-face, and sewn to the attached welt (Figure 116).

*Figure 117. Pillow with inserted welt cut straight
across the stripes.*

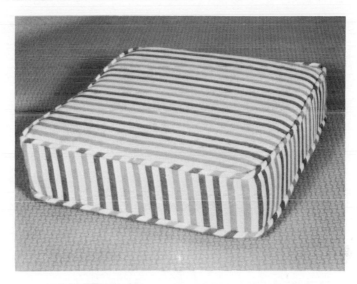

Figure 118. Pillow with inserted welt cut on the bias.

Questions

1. What is welt?
2. Why should welt strips not be cut directly from the roll of material?
3. How wide should welt strips be cut?
4. How should welt strips be cut from wide striped material?
5. Name two methods for cutting welt strips from narrow-striped material.

METALINE NAIL TRIM

Metaline nails are available in many colors, designs, and finishes and are, therefore, compatible with various types and styles of coverings. While these nails can have either solid brass or steel heads, experienced manufacturers and upholsterers believe it wise to use the solid-brass-headed metaline nails. The slight difference in cost is offset by the protection that brass nails afford against rusting and tarnishing and against the resultant discoloration of finished furniture. Besides the standard finishes, special finishes made by experts to meet unusual requirements are also available.

Metaline nails may be used on upholstered furniture for several purposes. They are frequently used to attach gimp to furniture or for purely decorative purposes (Figure 119).

93

Figure 119. French provincial chair with metaline nails placed head-on-head.

Tools and Equipment

Hammer

Materials

Metaline nails

Procedure

1. *Metaline Nails Placed Head-on-Head.*

On many modern and provincial pieces of furniture the metaline nail is used as a fundamental of design, and to emphasize the smart and straight lines of the furniture. Because metaline nails are decorative, they must be put on with great precision, and when driven in head-on-head, care must be taken that the heads follow the contour of the furniture (Figure 119).

2. *Spacing Metaline Nails.*

When metaline nails are spaced apart, it is very important that the spacings between the nails be all the same distance.
- Determine the desired distance between the nailheads.
- Cut a piece of cardboard to the width of the desired distance between each nailhead.
- Drive the first nail in halfway.
- Hold the cardboard under the head of the nail.
- Drive the second nail in halfway.
- Pull the cardboard out, and continue to the next nail (Figure 120).
- After all the metaline nails have been spaced, they can then be driven all the way down.

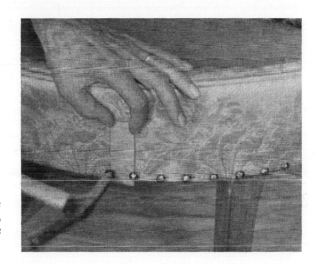

Figure 120. A piece of cardboard used to equalize the spacing of metaline nails.

Questions

1. For what purpose are metaline nails usually used?
2. What is used as a measuring device to space metaline nails?

GIMPING

Gimp is used to cover the upholstery tacks that fasten covering material to exposed woodwork. It is made in many colors and materials, so that there is gimp to match any kind of covering material.

While solid color gimp is used most often, it also comes in a mixture of colors for use with multicolored material. Gimp is

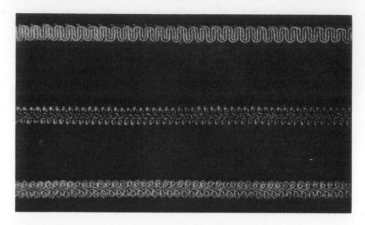

Figure 121. Three different weaves of gimp.

available in cotton, rayon, silk, or a combination of these. It is advisable *never* to use cotton gimp on silk, nylon, or rayon coverings, since the cotton gimp will fade more readily than the covering and the colors will no longer match.

Gimp is available also in various weaves, but the scroll gimp (top pattern, Figure 121), which has a more solid weave, is most popular. This weave is especially practical when the gimp is glued on, because it prevents the glue from coming through the openings in the weave.

Gimp may be purchased in various department stores by the yard or in 36-yard pieces.

There are three methods of attaching gimp to furniture:
1. With gimp tacks
2. With metalline nails
3. With glue

Tools and Equipment

Hammer

Materials

Gimp tacks; metalline nails; or glue

Procedure

1. *Attaching Gimp with Gimp Tacks.*
   • When tacking on gimp with gimp tacks, extreme care must be taken so as not to mar the finished woodwork.

96

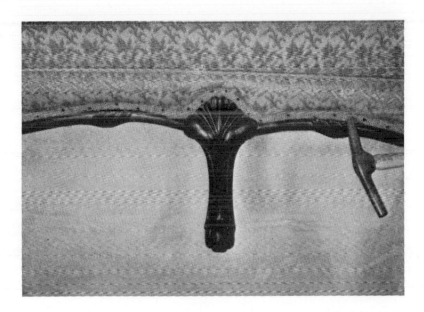

Figure 122. Gimp put on with gimp tacks.

- On straight lines the gimp tacks should be placed about 3 to 5 inches apart, and should be staggered, one tack on the outer edge of the gimp, and the next tack on the inner edge (Figure 122). This procedure will prevent the gimp from curling upward.
- To turn square corners, a gimp tack is tacked to the extreme outer edge of the gimp, directly in the corner. Fold the gimp into a miter pleat, and tack a gimp tack on the inner edge over the pleat.

Figure 123. Gimp put on furniture with glue.

Figure 124. Attaching gimp with metaline nails.   *Figure 125. Attaching gimp with glue.*

- On curves, or round pieces, tack the gimp on the extreme outer edge, and fold small pleats where necessary, and tack the inner edge of the gimp over the pleats.

2. *Attaching Gimp with Metaline Nails (Figure 124).*
   When tacking on gimp with metaline nails, care must be taken that the metaline nails are all spaced evenly apart. For spacing metaline nails, see Figure 120.

3. *Attaching Gimp with Glue.*
   - Gluing on gimp is a simple, but slow process. The gimp must be glued on evenly and neatly without getting any glue on the covering. The most popular glue for attaching gimp to furniture is white in color so that it is easy to see what has been glued. When it dries, this glue is transparent and, therefore, especially suitable for gluing open or laced gimp. See Figure 121.
   - Tack the end of the gimp at the starting point, and with a flat, narrow strip of wood, or a narrow strip of heavy cardboard, put the glue onto about 6 to 8 inches of the gimp (Figure 125). With large tacks, temporarily tack the gimp in place. and put glue on another 6 to 8 inches. Follow this procedure all along.

Questions

1. Name three methods of attaching gimp.
2. How should gimp tacks be placed on straight lines?
3. How should gimp tacks be placed on corners?
4. How is gimp attached with glue?

FABRIC SKIRTS

Fabric skirts are very popular on bedroom furniture as well as on modern and traditional living room pieces. There are four distinct styles of fabric skirts. The type selected is largely determined by individual preference, but some consideration should be given to the type of covering used on the furniture and to the size of the piece of furniture the skirt is to be put on.

For bedroom chairs with high legs, which are usually covered with a light fabric, a shirred skirt is very appropriate. On living room furniture with short legs, and a heavier covering, a box or kick pleat would be more suitable.

The popular types of fabric skirts are as follows:

The shirred fabric skirt (Figure 126)
The spaced box-pleat skirt (Figure 129)
The joined box-pleat skirt (Figure 132)
The kick-pleat skirt (Figure 135)

Figure 126. The shirred fabric skirt.

Shirred Fabric Skirt

The shirred skirt (Figures 126 & 161) is particularly appropriate on furniture which is covered with a delicate type of fabric, such as chintz, cretonne, or drapery material, since this type of material may be shirred easily.

Tools and Equipment

Sewing machine; shears; curved needle

Materials

Cover; welt cord; sewing twine

Procedure

1. *Making the Shirred Skirt.*
   * Determine the height of the skirt desired, allowing enough for a hem at the bottom.
   * Cut enough pieces of covering for the skirt to reach around the furniture about 2½ times. Although the material for this type of skirt may consist of a number of pieces joined together, each piece must be cut in the same direction, so that none of the floral designs will be crosswise.
   * Sew all the pieces together into one long strip.
   * Sew a hem all around the bottom edge.
   * Sew a draw or basting stitch all along the top edge of the skirt (Figure 127).

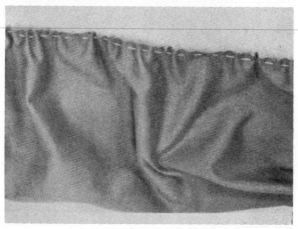

Figure 127. Drawstring stitched to the top of the skirt.

100

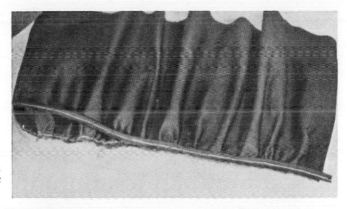

Figure 128. Welt sewn over the top edge of the shirred skirt.

- Shirr the skirt on the drawstring until the amount is shirred to reach around the furniture.
- Sew the shirring down ¼ inch from the top of the skirt.
- Sew a welt over the shirred top (Figure 128). For welting, see page 89.

2. *Attaching the Shirred Skirt.*
   - Measure the distance from the floor to the height of the skirt desired.
   - Draw a line all around the furniture.
   - Blind-tack the skirt to the line. See page 79, Blind-Tacking Outside Coverings (or skip directly to the following step).
   - With a curved needle and twine, sew the welted skirt to the furniture.

Box-Pleat Skirt

Although there is no set rule for the width of the box pleats (Figure 129), all the pleats on a particular skirt must be the same width. The spaces between the pleats must also be the same width.

Procedure

1. *Cutting the Covering for Box Pleats.*
   - Determine the height of the skirt desired, allowing enough for a hem at the bottom.
   - Cut enough pieces of covering for the skirt to reach around the furniture about 2½ times. Although the pieces of covering for this type of skirt may consist of a number of pieces joined together (since the seams can be placed under the pleats),

101

Figure 129. The spaced box-pleat skirt.

the covering pieces must all be cut in the same direction, so that none of the pattern, nap, or threads in the covering will be crosswise.

• Sew all the pieces together into one long strip.
• Sew a hem all around the bottom edge.

2. *Laying Box Pleats.*

• Determine the width of the box pleats.
• Cut a piece of cardboard the width of the pleat desired. Use this cardboard as a measuring device for each pleat.
• Cut another piece of cardboard one half the width used for the pleats. Use this piece of cardboard as a measuring device for each spacing. All box pleats and spacings will, therefore, be the same width.
• Pin the pleats down, with the pins about 1 inch from the top edge. This will permit sewing the pleats down without sewing over the pins (Figure 130).
• Sew the pleats down close to the top edge, so that this sewing will be covered with the welt.
• Remove the pins and sew a welt over the pleats (Figure 131). See page 89, Welting.

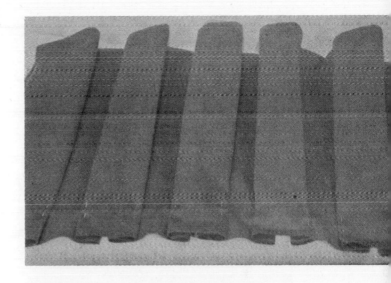

Figure 130. Spaced box-pleats properly pinned.

Figure 131. Welt sewn over the top edge of the spaced pleat.

3. *Attaching the Skirt.*
 • Measure the distance from the floor to the height of the skirt desired.
 • Draw a line all around the furniture.
 • Blind-tack the skirt to the line. See page 79, Blind-Tacking (or skip directly to the following step).
 • With a curved needle and twine, sew the welted skirt to the furniture.

103

Figure 132. The joined box pleat skirt.

Joined Box-Pleat Skirt

Procedure

1. **Cutting the Cover for Box Pleats**
   - Determine the height of the skirt desired, allowing enough for a hem at the bottom.
   - Cut enough pieces of covering for the skirt to reach around the furniture three times. Although the pieces of covering for this type of skirt may consist of a number of pieces joined together (since the seams can be placed under the pleats), the covering pieces must all be cut in the same direction, so that none of the pattern, nap, or threads in the covering will be crosswise.
   - Sew all the pieces together into one long strip.
   - Sew a hem around the bottom edge.

2. **Laying Box Pleats.**
   - Determine the width of the box pleats. Select a width that suits the piece of furniture, since no set width is required as long as each pleat is the same width as the others.
   - Cut a piece of cardboard to the determined width of the pleat.

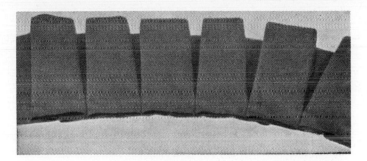

Figure 133. Joined box-pleats properly pinned.

Figure 134. Top edge of pleats sewn down with welt sewn to the top edge.

- Use this cardboard as a measuring device for each pleat to be certain that all the box pleats are the same width.
- Pin the pleats down, with the pins about 1 inch from the top edge to permit sewing the pleats down without sewing over the pins (Figure 133).
- Sew the pleats down close to the top edge, so that this sewing will be covered with the welt.
- Remove the pins and sew a welt over the pleats (Figure 134). See page 89, Welting.

3. *Attaching the Skirt.*
   - Measure the distance from the floor to the height of the skirt desired.
   - Draw a line all around the furniture.
   - Blind-tack the skirt to the line. See page 79, Blind-Tacking (or skip directly to the following step).
   - With a curved needle and twine, sew the welted skirt to the furniture.

105

Figure 135. The kick-pleat skirt.

Kick-Pleat Skirt

This type of skirt (Figure 135) is very popular in heavy, plain or small patterned coverings and on more massive types of furniture. It must be made so that the seams are covered on the corners.

Procedure

1. *Cutting the Covering for the Kick-Pleat Skirt.*
   - Determine the height of the skirt desired, allowing enough for a hem at the bottom.
   - Measure the exact distance across the front of the chair from corner to corner, and add 8 inches to this measurement.
   - Measure the exact distance across the sides, and across the rear of the chair from corner to corner. Add 8 inches to each measurement to allow for a 4 inch turn-under at each corner.
   - Cut four pieces of covering 8 inches wide (one for each cor-

ner). The height of these pieces must be the same as the height of the skirt pieces. Since the distance from corner to corner will vary, the coverings will have to be joined together as follows: side piece, corner piece, front piece, corner piece, side piece, corner piece, rear piece, corner piece.
- After all the pieces are joined together in their proper order, sew a hem around the bottom edge.

2. Laying Kick Pleats.
- Fold and pin the side piece to the center of the corner piece.
- Fold, and pin the front piece to the center of the same corner piece (Figure 136). Before sewing the pinned-up pleats, check

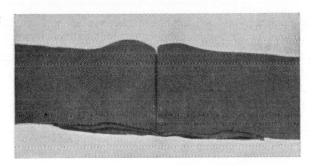

Figure 136. Kick-pleat properly pinned.

to make certain that all folds fit directly on the corners of the furniture.
- Repeat the first two steps on the remaining three corners.
- Sew the pleats down close to the top edge.
- Remove the pins and sew a welt over the top of the entire skirt (Figure 137). See page 89, Welting.

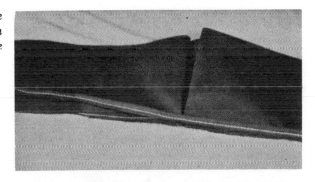

Figure 137. Top edge of pleat sewn down with welt sewn to the top edge.

3. *Attaching the Skirt.*
 • Measure the distance from the floor to the desired height of the skirt.
 • Draw a line all around the furniture at this height.
 • Blind-tack the skirt to the line. See page 79, Blind-Tacking (or skip directly to the following step).
 • With a curved needle and twine, sew the welted skirt to the furniture.

Questions

1. Name the four types of fabric skirts.
2. What type of skirt is most appropriate for a chair with high legs in a light fabric? for a short-legged piece in a heavy covering?
3. Why must covering pieces all be cut in the same direction?
4. What device is used to assure that all box pleats and spacings will be of the same width?
5. Explain how to measure a chair for a kick-pleat skirt.
6. In what order are the pieces of material for a kick-pleat skirt joined together?

Procedure 6.   Cushioning

Because furniture cushioning is so important to the comfort and appearance of a chair or sofa, special attention and care must be given to this procedure. After an explanation of the various cushioning materials such as feathers and down, polyfoam, cotton felt, and sponge rubber, there follow instructions on making cushions and on the more complicated cushioning devices, piping and tufting.

Feathers and Down

Feathers and down are not only the most luxurious and resilient of all cushion and upholstery fillings, but also the most practical and long lasting. They are mixed or blended together into various combinations to suit a particular need or purpose, for bedding, upholstering, and so on. The characteristics of the various feathers and down are as follows:

Down

Down (Figure 138) is the covering of young birds and the undercoating of older birds found next to the skin beneath the feathers. Down is especially thick on water fowl such as geese or ducks. Because the threadlike fibers radiate from a common center, down has practically no quill. It is not a part of any feather because feathers have a quill stem which is entirely absent in a

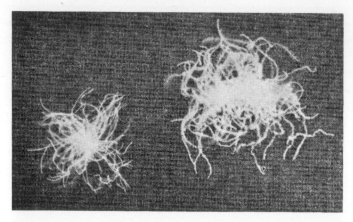

Figure 138. Down.

cluster of down. Pure down is scarce and expensive because only about 20 per cent of the entire amount of feather content obtained from one fowl is down.

Goose Feathers

The most valuable filling material after down is the goose feather (Figure 139). It is springy and buoyant due to its curved or cup-shaped contour and to the mass of long and slender fibers which grow from its curved quill. More of these fluffy fibers are found on goose feathers than on any other feather.

Figure 139. Goose feather.

Figure 140. Duck feather.

Duck Feathers

Duck feathers (Figure 140) are not quite so valuable as goose feathers for although they are arched and have a curved quill shaft, they do not possess the natural strength of goose feathers, nor the abundance of soft fibers.

Chicken and Turkey Feathers

These feathers have a low buoyancy because their contours are straight and flat. They should never be used in cushions and pillows where resiliency is desired, although the stripped and blown fibers from such feathers are frequently used as an adulterant of down.

Feather and Down Mixtures

For furniture cushion filling it is not necessary to use pure down, since feathers added to down give a cushion more buoyancy. Very good results can be obtained from mixtures containing anywhere from 25 to 75 per cent goose or duck feathers added to the down, depending upon the quality of the feathers used.

A grade of 75 per cent down and 25 per cent feathers makes an excellent cushion, and even 50 per cent down and 50 per cent feathers is very good. However, the more feathers used, the more the cushion will weigh.

Because feathers and down are sold by the pound, one should bear in mind that 1 pound of down goes much farther in filling a cushion than 1 pound of feathers.

For making a feather-and-down cushion casing see page 116.

111

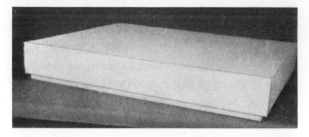

Figure 141. Polyfoam used on wood base upholstery.

Figure 142. Polyfoam cut for a chair back.

Figure 143. A shaped bolster of polyfoam.

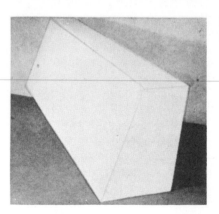

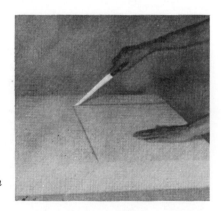

Figure 144. Cutting polyfoam with a large knife.

Polyfoam

Polyfoam is a new chemically developed foam which is especially adapted for use as a cushion filler and also for seats and furniture backs (Figures 141 & 142). In upholstery, polyfoam is used extensively for reversible cushions, Bahama lounges, mattresses, pillows, and bolsters (Figure 143).

Polyfoam is manufactured in a range of densities and comes in wide, thick slabs which have not only softness and resiliency, but also superior strength. While it is difficult to tear polyfoam, the slabs may be cut or sliced easily (Figure 144). Polyfoam can be cemented together with special cement and it adheres readily to metal, wood, and fabric. It is a good cushioning material because it is mildew-resistant and will not pack down or become brittle with use. Its light weight is another advantage; a slab 2 feet by 2 feet by 3 inches weighs less than 3 pounds.

Polyfoam is available in 1, 2, and 4 inch slabs, 24 by 72 inches in soft, medium, and firm densities.

Cotton Felt

On upholstered furniture, cotton felt is used chiefly to stuff spring-filled, loose cushions (Figure 145). It also is used over loose upholstery fillings to prevent dust, hair, or filling ends from coming through the cover. When put on properly, cotton felt will make a smooth job.

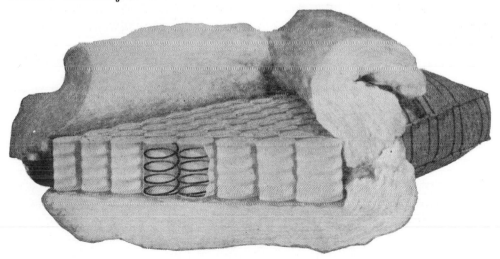

Figure 145. Cotton felt placed over a spring-filled loose cushion.

The cotton felt used in upholstery work is made from cotton linters which are a by-product from the cotton gin. After the long fibers are removed from the cotton bolls, the linters, particles which still cling to the seeds, are removed by a cutting process. The seeds may go through several cutting processes before all the linters are finally separated. The linters are then placed in a garnetting machine, where their fibers are combed out and woven into weblike sheets, layer upon layer, producing the cotton felt used by upholsterers and mattress makers. The various grades of cotton felt result from the various grades of linters. Upholsterers choose a quality of cotton felt suitable to the kind of work they are doing. Cotton felt comes in 15 pound rolls 27 inches wide. Although cotton felt is available in various thicknesses, the most commonly used thickness for upholstery is the 10- or 12-ounce cotton felt. The thickness of the cotton felt is determined by the weight per yard.

Sponge Rubber

Sponge, or foam, rubber is made of latex, which is the milk of the rubber tree, collected on plantations in Sumatra and Malaya and shipped to the United States in liquid form.

At the rubber-manufacturing plants, some chemicals are added to assist in curing and to resist aging, as well as to form a spongy structure. The latex is then whipped into a creamy froth, causing it to foam. The procedure is like making a huge cake, that is, the more air bubbles there are, the lighter and softer will be the finished product.

The material is then cured. After it has reached its proper consistency, it is poured into metal molds of various sizes and shapes, and placed into huge ovens to bake under heat and pressure. It is then taken from the molds, washed to remove all impurities, and dried. The result is a clean rubber cushion or pillow.

While sponge rubber is used extensively in mattresses and for public seating of all kinds, the furniture manufacturer, the upholsterer, and the home do-it-yourself man and woman also find it a pleasure to work with. The initial cost of foam rubber may seem to be somewhat high, but this investment is counterbalanced by a great number of advantages. Sponge rubber withstands hard usage over a long period of time. It is soft and resilient and will not mat down or lump. It is resistant to mildew and moths, and will not affect allergic persons as will some other stuffing.

Sponge rubber is available in various forms and sizes.

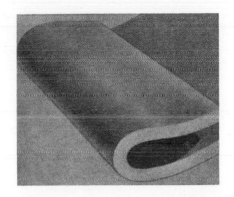

Figure 146. Flat solid-slab form sheet.

Flat Solid-Slab Sheets

The flat solid-slab sheets (Figures 146 & 147) are available in thicknesses varying from ¼ to 2 inches, and may be obtained in medium and firm densities. This slab-form sheet is most practical and economical for use on dining-room chair seats, benches, and headboards (Figure 212) since it can be cut to any size and shape (Figure 147). The remnants may be cemented together with a special cement made for this purpose.

Figure 147. Cutting the flat solid-slab form sheet to size.

Figure 148. Marking off core stock prior to cutting.

Cored Stock

Cored stock is made with molded openings on one side, and is used where more depth and resiliency are required. It is available in several thicknesses from 1 to 4½ inches, and can be cut, shaped, and cemented to make reversible cushions of any shape or size (Figure 148).

Full-Molded Inner Cushions

Full-molded units (Figure 149) have been molded ready to fit into the furniture. This type of cushion needs nothing more

115

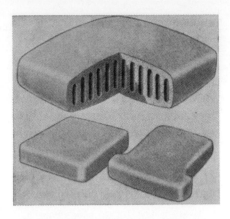

Figure 149. Full-molded inner cushions.

than a cover. There are many standard sizes and shapes available to fit a great number of pieces of furniture. Odd sizes can be made to individual specifications.

Rubber Pillows

Rubber pillows (Figure 198) too, may be obtained in molded form in most department stores. They are available in various sizes and shapes, the most popular being 12 inches, round or square, with a 2 inch border.

MAKING AND FILLING DOWN-AND-FEATHER-FILLED CUSHION CASING

When making feather-and-down-filled cushions for overstuffed chairs or davenports, it is necessary to have an inner casing for the feathers and down to prevent the down from coming through the upholstery covering.

This inner casing should be made with inner walls through the casing so that the feathers and down do not all shift to the front or back when the cushion is depressed.

The inner casing, made either of mattress ticking or heavy sateen, should be made 1 inch larger than the outer cushion covering to allow filling out all corners of the cushion.

Tools and Equipment

Sewing machine; shears; chalk; needle

Materials

Casing material; thread; feathers and down

116

Procedure

1. *Measuring Size of Casing.*
   - Measure the front (widest part of the chair) from arm to arm.
   - Measure the depth (rear corner to extreme front) of the required seat.

2. *Cutting Casing to Size.*
   Cut two pieces of casing material 1 inch larger than the measured size.

3. *Cutting Casing to Shape*
   - Lay one piece of the casing material in the chair.
   - Mark off the material for shape.
   - Cut out as marked, allowing 1 inch all around. This allowance will be $\frac{1}{2}$ inch for seams, and $\frac{1}{2}$ inch for fullness.
   - Lay the shaped piece of covering (face to face) on the other cut piece, and cut the lower piece of covering out to the same shape as the upper piece.
   - Cut out a border for the cushion 4 inches wide, and long enough to reach all around the cushion. This cushion border may consist of a number of pieces joined together.
   - Cut two pieces of covering for the inner walls of the casing 4 inches wide, and long enough to reach across the casing from side to side.

4. *Marking the Casing for Walls or Sections.*
   - Measure the casing front to back.
   - Divide the number by 3.
   - Draw two lines across the inside of each casing piece, equalizing the spaces (Figure 150).

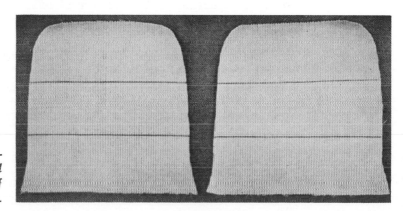

Figure 150. Cushion casing, top and bottom, marked off for center partitions.

117

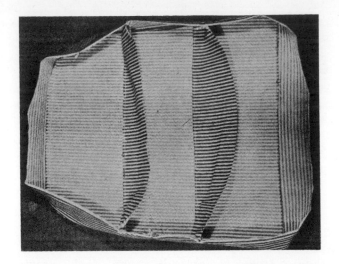

Figure 151. Cushion casing with center partition and border sewed to one side.

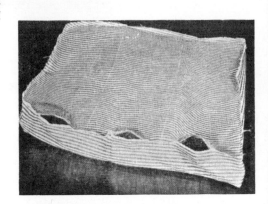

Figure 152. Cushion casing ready for filling.

5. *Sewing the Casing.*

- Join together the pieces for the border.
- Sew the border all around the top piece.
- Sew the two wall sections to the casing, directly on the marked lines (Figure 151).
- Sew the top of the wall sections to the other piece of the casing directly on the lines marked.
- Sew the border all around, leaving an opening at each section for filling. The border seams will be on the outside of the casing, since the casing cannot be turned inside out with the walls sewed in (Figure 152).

6. *Filling the Casing.*

Fill each section of the casing with feathers and down. It is advisable to fill the front sections of the casing a little firmer

118

than the middle and rear sections, thus, giving a better shape to the cushion as well as making a more comfortable seat. Sew the openings in the casing firmly together.

Questions

1. Why should an inner casing be made when cushions are filled with feathers and down?
2. What covering material should be used for a casing?
3. Why are inner walls put into a casing?
4. Why should the inner casing be made larger than the outer cushion cover?

MAKING LOOSE CUSHIONS FOR OVERSTUFFED FURNITURE

In repairing or recovering furniture cushions, the best way to make a cushion casing is to trace the shape of the old covering. When this method is used, however, care must be taken to be sure to stuff the chair arms and back as they were before, otherwise the cushion may be too large or too small.

It is best to make the cushion casing after the chair has been completed, or at least after the arms and back have been upholstered. A better fitting cushion will be the result.

Tools and Equipment

Sewing machine; chalk; shears; yardstick or tapeline; thread

Materials

Covering; welt cord

Procedure

1. *Measuring Cushion Cover.*
   - Measure the front (widest part of the chair) from arm to arm.
   - Measure the depth (rear corner to the extreme front).

2. *Cutting the Cushion-Top Covering to Rough Size.*
   Cut two pieces of covering, one for the cushion top, and one for the cushion bottom. This will permit the cushion to be reversible. Be sure to center any pattern or stripe.

119

Figure 153. Loose cushions on overstuffed furniture.

3. *Cutting the Cushion Top to Shape.*

- Lay one of the cut pieces in the chair, centering any pattern or stripe, and making certain that any nap or pattern is in the proper direction, front to back.
- Chalk the cushion top all around for size and shape.
- Cut the cushion top for shape, allowing ½ inch all around for seams.
- Lay this shaped piece of cushion top face-to-face onto the other cut piece, again taking care that the fronts, center patterns, or stripes match.
- Cut this piece to the same shape and size as the upper piece.

4. *Cutting the Cushion Border.*

Cut the border for the cushion about 4 inches deep, and long enough to reach around the cushion. This border may be pieced together of remnant goods, but one piece of border should be cut long enough (and cut in the same direction as the cushion tops) to cover the front of the cushion without having a seam in the front border.

5. *Cutting the Welt for the Cushion.*
Where welt is to be used around the cushion between seams, cut two strips of covering 1½ inches wide and long enough to reach around the cushion. See page 89, Welting.

6. *Sewing the Cushion.*
 • Join all the 4 inch pieces of border together into one strip.
 • Sew the welt around both cushion tops.
 • Sew the border all around one cushion top, taking care that no seams of this border are in the front of the cushion. On striped material, the stripes on the front border must match the stripes on the cushion tops.
 • Sew the other cushion top to the border.
    When the cushion is to be stuffed by hand, and an inner cushion spring with cotton felt is used as a filler, it will be necessary to leave the rear and both sides of the cushion open. Sew this cushion top to the border across the front only, and about 2 inches on each side (Figure 154). When the cushion is to be stuffed with a foam-rubber filler, the border may be sewn along the sides to about 2 inches from the rear of the cushion, since this type of filler may be folded into the casing (Figure 157).

7. *Stuffing the Cushion with Inner Spring and Cotton Filler.*
 • Place enough cotton felt into the casing to cover the bottom of the cushion. The number of layers of cotton felt needed will depend on the thickness of each layer and the quality of the cotton itself.
 • Place the inner spring over the cotton felt (Figure 154).
 • Place the same amount of cotton felt that was used on the bottom of the cushion, over the spring (Figure 155).
 • Work the filling and the spring firmly toward the front of the cushion.
 • With large pins (Figure 156) temporarily pin the cushion top to the border, and, with a curved needle and twine, sew the cushion shut.

121

Figure 154. Bottom of cushion filled with inner spring in place.

Figure 155. Cotton felt placed over the inner spring. Cushion ready to be pinned.

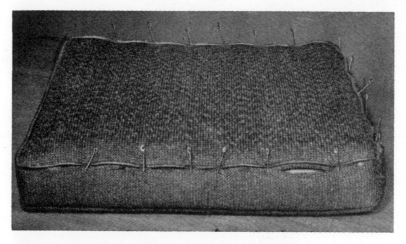

Figure 156. Cushion pinned, ready to be sewn shut.

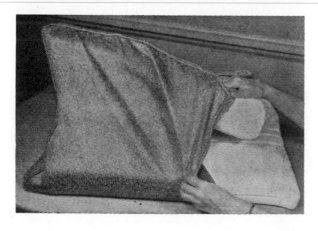

Figure 157. Inserting a foam rubber filler into the casing.

8. *Stuffing the Cushion with Foam Rubber or Polyfoam.*
   - Fold the filler over carefully.
   - Insert the filler into the casing (Figure 157).
   - Carefully unfold the filler in the casing.
   - With large pins, as in Figure 156, temporarily pin the cushion top to the border, and, with a curved needle and twine, sew the cushion shut.

Questions

1. Why must three sides of the cushion top be left open when filling the cushion with an inner spring and cotton felt filler?
2. How much of the cushion must be left open when filling it with foam rubber?

LOOSE CUSHIONS WITH REMOVABLE COVERS

Loose cushions with removable covers (Figure 158) usually have a filler of foam rubber or Polyfoam (Figure 159). They are used extensively on rattan and fiber furniture as well as on the open-arm frame construction.

This type of cushion is usually covered with the same material all around. However, a most interesting combination of colors and

Figure 158. Variety of loose cushions with removable covers.

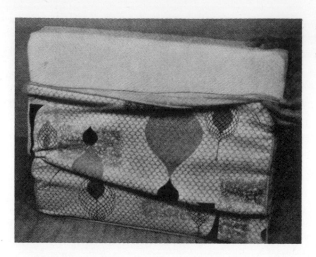

Figure 159. Inserting the filler into the cushion.

coverings may be used by having plain material for one side of the cushion and figured material for the other side. The borders and welt then are usually made from the plain material (Figure 159).

In the event that the cushions are covered with a bright-colored fabric which is to be laundered or dry-cleaned frequently, it is best to insert a zipper in the rear of the seat cushion and on the bottom of the back cushion.

Procedure

1. *Cutting the Cover for the Seat Cushion.*
   - Cut one piece of cover to the size and shape of the seat. Allow ½ inch for a seam all around. The pattern of figured material should run toward the rear. Make certain that the pattern in the cut cushion top is directly in the center.
   - Lay this cushion top cover face-to-face on the material and cut another piece for the cushion bottom, making certain that the pattern also runs in the proper direction. If more than one cushion is to be covered with the same patterned material, it is advisable to lay this cut figured top on all figured top pieces of the material. This procedure will assure centering and matching the pattern on all cushion tops.

2. *Cutting the Borders for the Seat Cushions.*
   - Cut the cushion borders. The height will depend on the thickness of the cushion (usually about 4 inches). The border must be long enough to reach around the front and both sides. Although this border may consist of a number of pieces, one

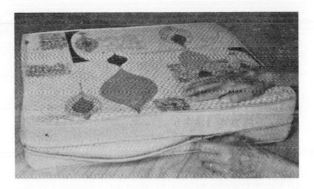

Figure 160. Closing the cushion with a zipper inserted in the border.

piece should be long enough to reach around the front, so that there will be no seam in the front of the cushion border.

- Cut two pieces of border 3 inches wide, and long enough to reach across the rear of the cushion, plus 4 inches to reach around each rear corner. These two pieces are used for the zipper opening (Figure 160).

3. *Making the Welt.*
Cut enough welt strips 1½ inches wide to reach around both cushion tops. See page 89, Welting.

4. *Sewing the cushion.*
- Sew the welt all around both cushion tops.
- Sew a ¾ inch seam across the length of the two 3 inch pieces of border. Then sew a zipper between these two border pieces, with the seams of these borders butting on each other to conceal the zipper.
- Lay the ends of this border with the zipper inserted, on the ends of the front-and-sides border. Trim off any surplus amount of material on each side, thus having the zipper directly in the center of the rear border.
- Join all the borders together end-for-end. The border should be so planned that the front of the cushion border will have no seam, and that the rear seat border with the zipper inserted will be centered (Figure 160).
- Sew the joined borders all around one of the cushion tops.
- With the zipper opened part way, sew the other side of the cushion border to the other cushion top. Make certain that the corners on both cushion tops are square in line.
- Turn the cushion right side out and insert the filler (Figure 159). Close the zipper.

125

5. *Making the Back Cushion.*
The back cushions are made by following the same procedures as those used for the seat cushions. However, the patterned material is cut with the pattern running toward the top, and the zippered border should be on the bottom of the back cushion. These same procedures may be followed for making slip covers for loose cushions.

Questions

1. Why is it advisable to insert a zipper in certain cushion covers?
2. How much material should be cut for the zipper opening?
3. What procedure is followed in making a back cushion as opposed to making a seat cushion?

PIPING

Piping or "fluting" is used extensively on barrel chairs, fanbacks, kidney-shaped chairs, and davenports with hollow-shaped backs (Figure 161). It gives upholstery a comfortable hollow shape for the back, because each pipe is stuffed individually and forms only a small curve in the back.

Pipes are frequently straight up and down (Figure 162) except in fan-back upholstery or in corners of kidney-shaped furniture (Figure 161) where the top of the pipe is wider.

Tools and Equipment

Hammer; shears; curved needle; regulator; pins

Materials

Cover; stuffing; stitching twine; tacks

Procedure

1. *Marking Positions for the Pipes on the Back.*
   • Locate the center of the back, top, and bottom.
   • Determine how many pipes are desired.
   • Mark off the pipes across the top. On straight backs (Figure 162), the pipes are the same width top and bottom, while on fanback chairs, or in the corners of kidney-shaped furniture (Figure 161), the three corner pipes are narrower at the bottom. On the latter, it will be necessary to taper the pipes.

126

Figure 161. *Kidney-shaped love seat with piped back and arms.*

Figure 162. *Straight back chair with piped back.*

Figure 163. Pipes marked off on the job.

- Mark off the pipes across the bottom.
- Draw a heavy pencil line from top to bottom for each pipe (Figure 163).

2. *Cutting the Covering for the Pipes.*
   - Measure the height of the pipe, allowing enough for the cover to reach over the top, and through the bottom of the back.
   - Measure the width of the pipes, allowing for the fullness desired in each pipe, plus ½ inch on each side of the pipe for sewing. Since the end pipe is usually tacked to the rear of the frame, allowance must be made when cutting the width of the cover for the two end pipes.
   - Cut as many pieces of covering as there are pipes. When the pipe has a tapered shape, it is important that the tapering is done on each side of the covering for each pipe. This will keep the pattern or pronounced weave straight up and down.

3. *Sewing the Pipe Covering.*
   Join all the cut and shaped pipe coverings together with a ½ inch seam. In the event that different sizes and shapes are marked off on the job, care must be taken that the pipe coverings are joined together in the same manner as those marked off on the job.

128

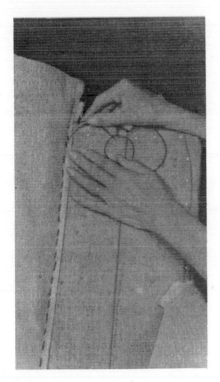
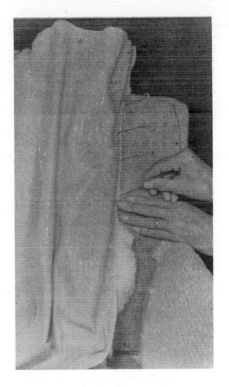

Figure 164. Sewing the center seam of the pipe covering to the center line of the job.

Figure 165. The seam on the covering pinned directly on the line marked off on the job.

4. *Sewing the Joined Pipe Covering to the Job.*
Sew one seam of the center pipe covering to the job. The center pipe is now ready for stuffing (Figure 164).

5. *Stuffing the Pipes.*
• Twist cotton felt into a roll to the firmness desired. On tapered pipes it will also be necessary to taper the cotton felt on the bottom.
To assure that all the pipes are of equal firmness it is best to measure and make a note of the amount of cotton felt used in the center pipe, and stuff the same amount of cotton felt in all the other pipes.
• Fill the center pipe with the rolled-up cotton felt (Figure 165).
• Pin the seam on the cover directly on the next line (Figure 165).

129

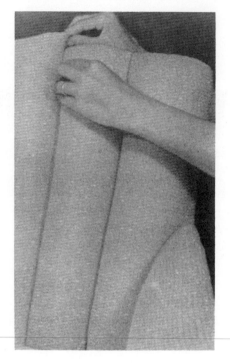

Figure 166. Seam on the covering sewn directly on the line marked off on the job.

Figure 167. Folding a pleat with the balance of covering left on the side of the pipe.

- Sew the seam on the line (Figure 166) and fill the next pipe. Follow this procedure until all the pipes are filled.
- Fill the end pipes, tacking the covering to the outside of the frame.

6. *Finishing the Tops of the Pipes.*
   - Fill the desired amount of stuffing to the top of each pipe.
   - Pull the cover over and tack the center of the pipe cover to the outside of the top back.
   - Pull down the cover on the top sides of each pipe, folding a pleat with the balance of the cover left on each side of the pipe (Figure 167).

130

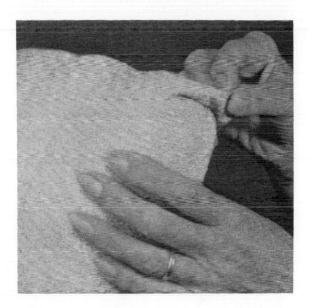

*Figure 168. Laying the end pleat
directly on the corner of the job.*

7. *Finishing the Top of the End Pipe.*
   Lay one pleat directly on the corner (Figure 168) with the pleat
   laying downward.

Questions

1. Why should the cover for each pipe be cut wider than it is
   marked off on the job?
2. What seam allowance should be made for sewing the pipes
   together?
3. How should the pleats on each pipe be laid?
4. How should the pleats on the corner end pipe be laid?

TUFTING

Tufting furniture is the upholsterer's art. Although it is not
too difficult, it should be done with caution, patience, and a lot of
practice before cutting into any actual covering material.

When re-covering tufted furniture, it is advisable to remove
the old covering carefully, and take note of the sizes of tufts
marked off on the covering. After the filling is removed, again take
note of the size of the tufts marked off on the job. This will give
the proper covering allowance for the tufts.

131

The filling for tufting may be Kapok, Polyfoam, foam rubber, or curled hair. When curled hair is used, a layer of cotton felt must be placed over the hair, so that the hair will not come through the covering.

The latter method is the most difficult for the beginner, since the hair must be laid evenly, and the cotton felt must also be placed so that there will be no lumps in the tufts.

The most popular shape in tufting is the diamond which is formed by the four buttons at its corners and the pleats at its sides. Usually, the longer dimension of the diamond is vertical, and the shorter dimension horizontal (Figure 169).

The size of the tuft is determined by the size of the job being tufted. On large overstuffed davenports or chairs (Figure 169) the tufts should be larger and deeper than on the smaller tufted-back chairs.

To visualize how the job will appear with various sizes of tufts, it is a good policy to experiment first with large-headed upholstery tacks until the desired size of diamond tuft is determined.

Figure 169. Davenport with diamond-shaped tufted back.

Tools and Equipment

Hammer; shears; regulator; needle

Materials

Stuffing; cover; stitching twine; tacks

Procedure

1. *Marking the Positions for the Tufts on the Job.*
   - Determine the size of the diamond.
   - Locate the exact center of the width on the job.
   - Determine the distance of the first row of buttons from the top.
   - Draw a line across the job on the burlap covering for the top row of buttons.
   - Draw a second line below the first at a distance equal to the desired height of the diamond.
   - Mark off, on both lines, the width of the desired diamond. Start in the center so that the end buttons will be the same distance from each end.
   - With a ruler, draw a line diagonally both ways, from the markings on the first line to the markings on the second line. The meeting or crossing of these two diagonal lines will be the position for the second row of buttons, forming the diamond shape (Figure 170). On high backs, where more than three rows of buttons are necessary, repeat the process of markings for more rows of buttons.

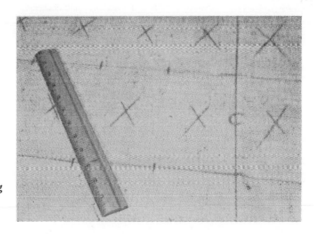

Figure 170. Marking the diamond-shaped tufts on the job.

133

Do not use chalk for the markings on the burlap since chalk lines will come off while filling the tufts. Use a soft-lead pencil, and be very exact in your measurements and markings. Differing as much as ¼ inch on one tuft, would mean reducing that tuft ¼ inch, and would enlarge the next tuft ¼ inch. The total difference of ½ inch from one tuft to another would be noticeable on the completed tuft.

2. *Determining the Cover Allowance for Each Tuft.*
   - The covering must be marked off with the same amount of buttons as are marked off on the job. However, the cover marks for buttons must be farther apart. This is called "cover allowance" and is determined by the depth of the tuft desired.
   - On the marked-off tufts on the job, tack or pin a narrow strip of cardboard to the top and to the bottom of the button mark. Make this cardboard strip long enough to correspond to the desired fullness of the tuft.
   - To determine the cover allowance for the width of this tuft, tack or pin another strip of cardboard to one of the marked-off buttons.
   - Raise this strip of cardboard until it meets the first cardboard strips at the center top, and tack or pin this end to the other side of the tuft (Figure 171).
   - Remove the cardboard strips, and carefully measure each strip at the tack hole. This measurement will be the size of the cover to be marked off for each tuft.

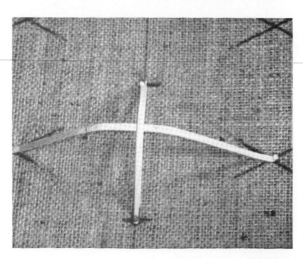

Figure 171. Determining the cover allowance for the tuft.

134

3. *Determining the Size of Covering Required.*
   - To determine the width of the required piece of covering, count the number of tufts crosswise. Multiply this by the width of covering required for each tuft. Add to this an allowance for the cover to reach around each end.
   - To determine the length or height of the required piece of covering, count the number of tufts up and down. Multiply this by the length of cover required for each tuft. Then add to this total an allowance for the cover to reach across the top and through the bottom of the back.

4. *Marking the Tufts on the Cover.*
   - Locate the exact center in the width of the covering.
   - Determine the distance of the first row of buttons from the top. Allow for filling to be placed into the top pipes (the tops and bottoms on tufted jobs are called pipes).
   - On the underside of the covering, draw a line across the cover for the top or first row of buttons.
   - Draw another line across the covering, the height of the diamond (the length of the long strip of cardboard).
   - Mark off on the two lines the width of the diamond or the length of the short strip of cardboard.
   - With a ruler, draw a line diagonally both ways from the markings on the first line to the markings on the second line. The meeting or crossing of these two lines will be the position for the second row of buttons, and will form a diamond shape on the covering. Again be very exact in the measurements and markings, since a small difference will increase or decrease the height of the stuffed tuft.

5. *Joining the Covering for Tufting.*
   - When the coverings are not wide enough, it will be necessary to add a piece of covering for the width required. The two pieces must be sewn together in a special way to prevent the seam from showing in the finished job.
   - Cut the covering in zigzag shape, corresponding with the shape of the diamonds (Figure 172).
   - Sew the pieces together. The seams will now be hidden in the pleats that lay diagonally between the buttons.

6. *Making Buttons for Tufting.*
   - In most cases, the buttons for tufting are covered with the same material as that used in the covering. Cut material from

Figure 172. Covering marked off and cut zigzag for joining.

remnants left over after cutting out larger pieces. Do not cut directly from the roll since this wastes material.
• See Figures 15 and 16 for making buttons by machine.

7. *Fastening Buttons to a Solid Wood Base.*
On a solid wood base, the buttons are tacked to the marked-off wood base. For this purpose use the tack button mold (*c,* Figure 16).

8. *Fastening the Buttons to a Webbing and Burlap Foundation.*
On open structures which have a webbing and burlap foundation, the buttons must be sewn on through the webbing and burlap, and then tied to the rear of the job. For this purpose, use either the loop, or tuft button mold (*a* and *b,* Figure 16).
• Cut as many twines as there are buttons.
• String all the twines through the buttons.
• Thread both ends of the twine through a large straight upholsterer's needle (Figure 173).
• Stick the needle through the covering from the outer side exactly on the button marks which are on the underside of the covering.
• Stick the needle through the burlap, exactly on the button marks on the job. Both ends of the twine must come through the rear of the burlap.

136

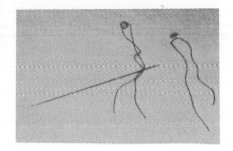
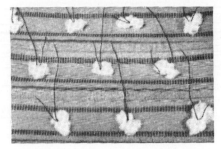

Figure 173.   Figure 174.

- Slipknot the two twines together in the rear. To prevent the knots of the twine from pulling through the webbing in the rear, place a small wad of cotton felt into the slipknot (Figure 174).

9. *Filling the Tufts.*
   - After the first row of buttons is fastened, place the filling into the first row of tufts.
   - Fasten the second row of buttons and fill this row, laying the pleats diagonally between the buttons. On backs, all pleats in each tuft are laid downward, and on seats the pleats in the tufts are all laid toward the front.
   - Continue until all the rows are filled.

10. *Filling the Pipes.*
    The tops and bottoms on tufted jobs are called pipes.
    - Fill the desired amount of stuffing on the top of each pipe.
    - Pull the cover over and tack the center of this pipe cover to the outside of the top back.
    - Pull down the cover on the top sides of each pipe, folding a pleat with the balance of the cover left on each side of the pipe.
    - Follow the same procedure at the bottom pipes, pulling the cover through at the bottom.

Questions

1. What is the first step in tufting?
2. In marking positions for buttons on covering, why must allowance be made?
3. What will determine the amount of allowance?
4. What will determine the type and color of buttons to be used?
5. How should pleats be laid on seats?
6. How should pleats be laid on backs?

137

Procedure 7.   Furniture Frames

CONSTRUCTING FRAMES

Anyone who wants to make his own frames for upholstery either on a production basis, or for only one frame, should be familiar with the most important steps and the materials to be used whether for a davenport, chair, or merely a footstool.

The following directions should be strictly adhered to in making the furniture illustrated and described in this book.

Procedure

1. *Kinds of Lumber for Frames.*
   The first step in frame manufacturing is selection of the proper kind of lumber, a step too often ignored because some people feel that "it's all covered anyway." For those parts of upholstered furniture frames which will be exposed (Figure 176), it is advisable to use walnut, mahogany, birch, gum, or pecan, since these woods can be beautifully finished.

   Lumber for frame-making that is not exposed (Figure 175) should be a dense, close-grained wood with a medium degree of hardness. Birch, soft maple, gum, or sycamore is ideal. The lumber must be soft enough for tacking without splitting the wood, and yet hard enough to hold the tacks permanently.

   The lumber used in the manufacture of frames should be well seasoned and preferably "kiln-dried." Green lumber should never be used because glue will not adhere to it, and it will warp and shrink.

138

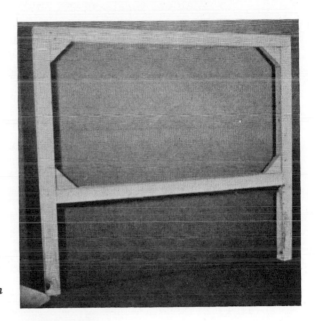

Figure 175. Frame construction where joints are covered.

Figure 176. Frame construction where joints are exposed.

2. Frame Assembly.

Nails should never be used in upholstery frame construction. Glue with either dowels or wood screws is the standard means of joint construction.

139

When the frame joint is covered with upholstery (Figure 175), flathead wood screws (Figure 22) may be used with good results. The screwheads should be countersunk in the wood so that they will not interfere with the covering. Where the frame joint is exposed (Figure 176), wood dowels are preferable (Figures 23 and 24) because the dowels can be sanded smooth and finished.

Questions

1. What kinds of lumber are suitable for exposed furniture frames? for unexposed frames?
2. What is the standard means of frame construction?

GLUING

One of the important steps in frame assemblage is the selection and proper use of glue and gluing procedures. There are various kinds of glue to choose from and each kind has its advantages and disadvantages.

Hot Glue

This type of glue is made by soaking animal-hide glue in flakes or granular form in hot water, and heating it in a double-boiler gluepot. This is the type of glue commonly used in school shops and production plants. Although it is considered the best type of glue in many ways, hot glue has disadvantages for the small-shop worker. It must be applied at a certain heated temperature and must not be used on cold lumber, since it will jell immediately. Then, too, it congeals rapidly, leaving little time for fitting or making changes while the glued stock is being placed in clamps.

Liquid Glue

Perhaps the most commonly used glue for the small shop or home-shop worker is liquid fish or animal glue which can be purchased in small cans, ready to use. This type of glue has many advantages to the small-shop worker, and, when used as directed, will be as strong as the wood itself. It dries slowly, allowing ample time to put the frame pieces together. Liquid glue may be purchased in various size cans to suit different needs.

Casein Glue

The most popular type of glue for outdoor furniture and marine work is casein (waterproof) glue, which is especially recommended for furniture that is subjected to outdoor weather or extremely damp climate.

Casein glue sets slowly, giving the worker ample time to fasten his clamps. Because casein glue comes in powder form, it must be prepared daily, following the directions on the box for proper consistency.

Questions

1. What are the disadvantages of hot glue?
2. What are the advantages of liquid and casein glue?

FINISHING FRAMES

It is advisable to finish all exposed wood before the furniture is upholstered, to avoid the risk of getting stain or finishing material on the covering.

After all the exposed parts of the wood frame have been thoroughly sanded, they are ready to be stained. Before staining, it is extremely important to clean off any glue which may have adhered to the wood, since glue will not absorb stain.

Because stains are available in a variety of colors, the choice should be determined by the color of the furniture already in the room. Two types of stains generally are used—water stain and oil stain.

Water Stain

This is perhaps the most popular stain because it can be purchased in powder form and mixed with water to the shade desired, and the amount needed.

1. *Mixing Water Stain.*
   When mixing this stain, it is advisable to mix a little more than the required amount because if you run short, the second mixing may not turn out to be the exact same color as the first. Because it is so difficult to match the colors in two mixings, always mix an ample amount the first time.

2. *Finishing with Water Stain.*

- Before applying the stain to the furniture, apply a little stain first to another piece of wood. Should the color be too light, add more stain to the mixture; should the color be too dark, add more water. This will assure the proper color before staining the furniture.
- To overcome the grain raising caused by water stain, sponge the wood first with water, permitting the grain to raise.
- After the wood is dry, sand it carefully.
- Dust the wood completely.
- Apply the stain.

Oil Stain

Oil stain may be purchased in various size cans or bottles, and in a vast variety of colors, ready to use.

1. *Finishing with Oil Stain.*

Oil stain is favored by many because it is easy to apply and results in many interesting tones which would not be possible with water stain. Also, oil stain does not raise the grain.

- Apply the stain evenly with a brush or spray gun.
- When the stain has had time to penetrate the wood, wipe away excess stain to obtain an even color throughout.
- Allow 24 hours for the stain to dry.
- Apply a wash coat of shellac to seal the stain allowing ½ hour for drying.
- On open-grain woods, apply a paste wood filler, following the manufacturer's directions. Wipe the wood, and allow the filler to dry completely. Sand lightly and wipe the wood off completely. Add a final coat of shellac.
- On close-grain wood, add a second coat of shellac.

Final Finishes

Three types of final finishes are most commonly used: shellac finish, varnish finish, and lacquer finish.

1. *Applying a Shellac Finish.*

On furniture where only the legs are to be finished, three or four coats of shellac, when properly applied, will provide an excellent finish.

142

- The first coat of shellac which will provide a base for further coats should be thinned considerably with alcohol. Because shellac dries quickly when applied, the worker should proceed briskly, brushing on the shellac with the grain of the wood. Avoid overbrushing.
- After the shellac has dried thoroughly, carefully rub the work with very fine sandpaper or very fine steel wool. Wipe the wood thoroughly.
- Brush on a second coat of shellac, but do not thin this coat as much as the first.
- Sand with fine abrasive and wipe the wood clean.
- Repeat the two previous steps until the desired finish is obtained.
- Apply a good floor wax for the final finish. The wax will protect the shellac finish, as well as bring out a beautiful luster.

2. *Applying a Varnish Finish.*
   Varnish, which is perhaps the most popular finish, provides an excellent luster and is easily applied. However, unless a high quality material is used, varnish will, in time, check and crack making it necessary to refinish the furniture. Varnishes are available in high-gloss, semigloss, and dull-stain finishes, the latter of which is the most popular. Because varnishes dry very slowly, extra precautions should be taken to have the furniture in a dustproof room for drying. The varnishing procedure is as follows:
   - Apply a sealing coat of varnish with a brush.
   - Allow the varnish to dry thoroughly.
   - Sand the surface with very fine abrasive or steel wool.
   - Wipe the surface completely clean.
   - Repeat these steps until the desired finish is obtained, allowing more time for drying after each coat.
   - Wax the surface with a good furniture or floor wax.

3. *Applying a Lacquer Finish.*
   Lacquer finishes are now used to a great extent by furniture manufacturers since they provide an exceptionally durable finish that will not mar nor crack easily. The most satisfactory way of applying lacquer is with an air brush. However, because lacquer dries quickly, care must be taken not to repeat brush strokes. Lacquer is applied as follows:
   - Spray or brush on the first coat of lacquer, allowing about 2 hours drying time.

143

- Sand with very fine abrasive or steel wool and wipe clean.
- Repeat the first two steps, allowing 4 hours drying time.
- Apply a good furniture or floor wax.

Questions

1. When is it advisable to stain exposed wood?
2. Name the two most generally used types of stain?
3. Why is it advisable to mix more water stain than the required amount?
4. Name the three most commonly used final finishes?

ATTACHING LEGS

Tapered wooden legs are used extensively on modern furniture and in many other ways. They may be obtained from hardware stores as well as from building supply dealers in 3- to 28-inch heights. The 3-, 4-, and 5-inch legs have a ¾-inch satin brass ferrule, while the larger sizes have a 2-inch ferrule (Figure 177). Each leg has a glider attached to the bottom, and a machine screw set in the top.

While these legs are available in a variety of finishes, the majority are sold unfinished permitting the user to finish the legs to suit his own preferences, or to match the finish to other furniture in the room.

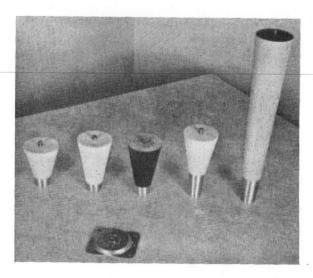

Figure 177. Legs for modern furniture.

Procedure

1. *Selecting the Proper Size Leg.*
   The height of the leg to be used is determined by the desired height of the completed piece. When replacing outmoded front legs on furniture (Figure 178), use the same height legs as those which were removed from the furniture (Figure 179), thus insuring the same backward tilt.

Figure 178. Chair with square tapered legs.

Figure 179. Same chair with round tapered legs.

2. *Fastening the Leg Plates.*
   - Fasten straight leg plates directly onto the corners of the furniture (Figure 180).
   - Fasten slant leg plates toward the inside from the outer edge (Figure 181) so that the leg will not extend out farther than the frame.

3. *Fastening the Legs.*
   Screw the legs into the plate (Figure 182).

Figure 180. Fastening the square flat attaching plate.

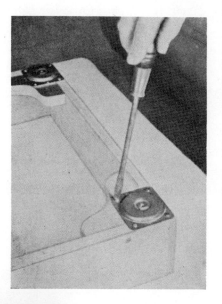

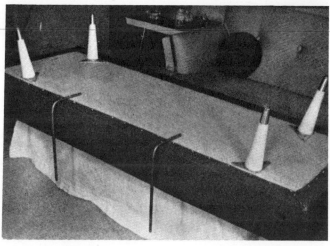

Figure 181. Legs fastened to angle plates.

146

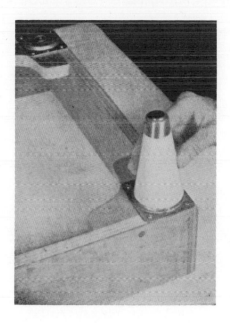

Figure 182. Turning the leg into the plate.

Questions
1. When replacing front furniture legs, why is it necessary to use the same height leg as was used previously?
2. How should slant leg plates be fastened and why?

3

JOBS

JOB 1. STOOL WITH SOLID BASE UPHOLSTERY

The stool shown in Figure 183 is very popular and easy to make. It can be covered and finished to blend in with all types of modern furniture and its light weight makes it easy to handle. Since this stool has a solid wood base on top, the filling should be a 4 inch slab of either foam rubber or Polyfoam (Figure 185). The wood frame is exposed and therefore, should be made of hardwood. Since the upholstery is simple and involves very little sewing, the corners can be sewn by hand if no sewing machine is available.

Material for the Frame

Quantity	Description	Thickness	Width	Length
2	Front boxings	1 inch	4 inches	18 inches
2	Side boxings	1 inch	4 inches	16 inches
4	Corner blocks	1 inch	3 inches	3 inches
1	Plywood top	¾ inch	18 inches	18 inches
	Legs with flat attaching plates			

1. *Assembling the Frame.*

Although the exact sizes of lumber are given in the bill of material, it is advisable to cut each piece a little larger. This will permit you to square off each piece before assembling the frame. After all the pieces of wood have been cut to size and squared off, assemble the frame as follows:

• Join the two side boxings to the inside outer edge of the front and rear boxings, making the frame 18 by 18 inches square. Since the corner joints in this frame will be exposed, the joints

151

Figure 183. Stool with solid board top upholstery.

should be fastened together with wood dowels and glue (see Constructing Frames, page 138.

- Bore a ¼-inch hole through the flat side of each corner block. This hole will accommodate the screw which is used to fasten the top to the frame (Figure 188).
- Attach the four corner blocks to the center of the boxing. Do not attach the iron attaching plates permanently at this time, because they would interfere with the screws for holding the board top through the holes in the corner blocks (Figure 184).

2. *Finishing the Frame.*
For finishing, see Finishing Frames, page 141.

Figure 184. Frame assembled with the corner plates temporarily fastened.

Figure 185. Filler placed on the board top.

152

3. *Cutting the Top Filler.*

Cut the top filler 19 by 19 inches. These dimensions will permit the filler to overhang ½ inch all around the board top (Figure 185) providing a squeeze-out on the filler and also insuring a firm fitting cover.

4. *Cutting the Cover.*

- Cut one piece of covering 30 by 30 inches square. This will allow enough cover for all sides, as well as for tacking the material to the bottom of the board top.
- Center the wood base on the underside of the cover. Then, with chalk, draw a line around the base and square off the corners. Cut out the four corner pieces, allowing ½ inch for scams (Figure 186).
- Sew up the four corners on the cover with ⅓-inch seams (Figure 187).

Figure 186. The cover cut to size with ½ inch allowance for seams.

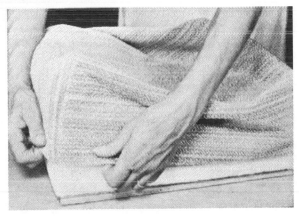

Figure 187. Stripping the sewn-up cover over the filler.

Figure 188. *Fastening the wood base to the frame with screws through the corner blocks.*

Figure 189. *The bottom of the frame with legs turned into place.*

5. *Covering the Board Top.*
  • Strip the sewn cover over the filler, making certain that the seams on the cover are directly on the corners of the wood base (Figure 187).
  • Tack the cover to the bottom of the wood base.
  • Fasten the covered wood top to the frame with screws through the corner blocks (Figure 188).
  • Attach the four iron plates permanently to the corners of the frame.
  • Turn in the four legs (Figure 189).

JOB 2. OPEN-LID STOOL

The open-lid stool (Figure 190) can be used as either a sewing or darning container as well as for many other useful purposes. Although the frame is entirely covered, the wood should be close-grained and of medium hardness (birch, soft maple, or gum), because the lumber must be soft enough to receive tacks without splitting the frame. The wood need not be No. 1 grained, however. Because the stool has a solid wood base with a hinged lid, the upholstery filler should be either foam rubber or a Polyfoam slab 2 inches thick. Since the upholstery for the lid covering involves very little sewing, the corners can be sewn by hand if a sewing machine is not available.

154

Figure 190. The open-lid stool.

Bill of Material

Quantity	Description	Dimensions	Part
1	Birch, soft maple or gum	1 x 6 x 20 inches	Front boxing
1	Birch, soft maple or gum	1 x 6 x 20 inches	Rear boxing
2	Birch, soft maple or gum	1 x 6 x 14 inches	Side boxings
1	Plywood	¾ x 20 x 16 inches	Lid
1	Plywood	½ x 20 x 16 inches	Bottom
2	Brass	1½ x 1 inches	Hinges
4	Any suitable wood	12 inches high	Legs
4	Steel	Flat, size to fit legs	Attaching plates

1. *Assembling the Frame.*

Although the exact sizes for the frame parts are given in the bill of materials, it is advisable to cut each piece a little longer. This will permit you to square off each piece before assembling the frame. After all the pieces of wood have been cut to size and squared off, assemble the pieces as follows:

• Join the two side boxings to the inside outer edge of the front and rear boxings, thus making the frame size 20 by 16 inches. Glue and flathead wood screws may be used. However, the screwheads should be countersunk so that they will not interfere with the covering.

• Fasten the ½-inch plywood to the bottom of the frame. This frame will not have corner blocks because they would interfere with the inside lining. The plywood bottom will keep the frame square.

155

Figure 191. *The lid attached to the frame.*

Figure 192. *Blind-tacking the end border.*

Figure 193. *Blind-tacking the border to the frame.*

- Fasten the four iron attaching plates for the legs to the bottom corners. The height of the completed stool is governed by the height of the legs used.
- To assure that the lid will fit squarely, fasten the hinges to the lid and to the top of the frame (Figure 191). The hinges are then removed until the stool is upholstered, after which they are again replaced, using the same holes for the screws.

2. *Upholstering the Boxing.*
    - Using a narrow strip of cardboard, blind-tack the two side borders to the top of the side boxings.
    - Tack these borders to the bottom, and to the front and rear of the frame (Figure 193).
    - Blind-tack the front and rear borders to the top of the front and rear boxings (Figure 193).

156

Figure 194. The border folded in place.

- Tack these borders to the bottom of the frame. The ends of these borders are turned under, with the fold directly on the corner of the frame (Figure 194).
- With a curved needle and heavy thread, sew the corners by hand.

Covering Required for the Stool

Quantity	Size	Description
2	22 x 10 inches	Front and rear boxings
2	18 x 10 inches	Side boxings
1	29 x 25 inches	Lid top
1	22 x 18 inches	Underside of the lid
1	1½ x 80 inches	Strips for welt

3. Cutting the Filler for the Lid.
Cut the top filler 21 by 17 inches out of 2-inch foam rubber or Polyfoam. This will permit the filler to overhang ½ inch all around the board top (Figure 185).

4. Cutting the Covers for the Lid.
- Cut one piece of cover 29 by 25 inches. This will allow enough cover for all sides, as well as for tacking the cover to the inside of the lid.
- Lay the lid on the underside of the cover, equalizing the overhang distance on all four sides. Chalk off the cover all around, and square off the corners. Cut the four corner pieces out, allowing ½ inch for seams (Figure 186).
- Sew up the four corners on the cover with ½ inch seams (Figure 187).

157

- Strip the sewn cover over the filler, making certain that the seams on the cover are directly on the corners of the lid (Figure 187).
- Tack the cover to the bottom of the lid.
- Tack the welt all around the extreme outer edge of the lid.
- Cut the cover for the underside of the lid, 22 by 18 inches.
- With large tacks or pins, baste the underlid piece of cover to the welt. The edges of this cover should be turned under all around.
- With a curved needle and heavy thread, sew the underlid cover to the welt.

5. *Lining the Inside of the Frame.*
   - Cut one 19 by 15-inch piece of lining material for the bottom. Muslin, cambric, or denim is very appropriate for the lining.
   - Cut the inside side lining 8 inches wide, and long enough to reach around the bottom piece. This may consist of a number of pieces joined together.
   - Join the side lining all around the bottom piece, forming a bag.
   - With the seams on the outside, drop the bag into the frame. Fold the top edges of the side lining under. Then tack or sew the lining to the inside, near the top inner edge. This will permit the bag to be shaken free from dust or particles without turning the stool upside down.

Figure 195. With the hinges back in place, cloth strips are tacked to the lid and inside of the frame.

- Attach the hinges.
- A strip of cloth, or a fine brass chain, tacked to the lid and on the inside of the frame will prevent the lid from tilting back too far and possibly loosening the hinges (Figure 195).

JOB 3. SQUARE AND ROUND TOSS PILLOWS

Toss pillows are a very versatile decorating device. They may be round or square, roll or bolster style, or a combination of all these shapes. They can be made in any color, texture, or pattern. Let your imagination run away with you and pile them on bedspreads, chairs, or davenports where they will add comfort as well as design (Figures 196 & 197).

Although toss pillows may be covered with the same material as that used in the upholstery, in most instances, toss pillows are covered with other types and colors of fabrics to blend or contrast with the colors used in the covering.

Figure 196. Square and round toss pillows.

Figure 197. Square and round toss pillows on a bahama lounge.

All the various types and colors of material for toss pillows are too numerous to mention. Some of the more popular fabrics are corduroy, damask, brocades, rep, terry cloth, and heavy-looped pile fabrics.

When selecting colors for toss pillows, the purpose of the pillows should be taken into consideration. Pillows used for decorative purposes only may be covered with a brighter and lighter shade, while pillows used frequently, such as headrests, should be of a darker shade.

Pillow bases of various shapes and sizes made of foam rubber or Polyfoam may be purchased ready to insert into the covered pillow without the use of casing material (Figure 198). The most popular sizes are the 12-inch square and the 12-inch round, with a 2-inch boxing all around.

1. *Making the Square Pillow.*
   - Cut two pieces of cover 1 inch smaller than the filler. This will make the cover fit snugly.
   - Cut enough border pieces to reach around the pillow. The width of this border will depend upon the thickness of the filler.
   - Cut enough welt strips to reach around both pillow tops. For welt, see page 89, Welting.

160

Figure 198. Shaped foam rubber pillows, ready to cover.

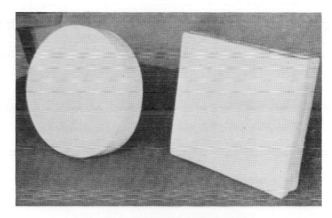

Figure 199. Sewing welt around a square pillow top.

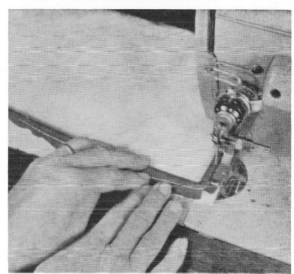

Figure 200. Inserting the filler into the casing.

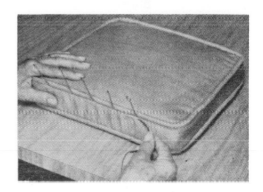

Figure 201. Closing the pillow with a curved needle.

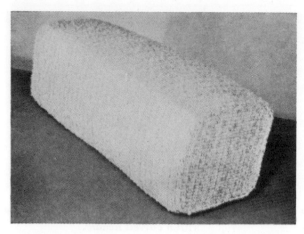

Figure 206. Bolster with square ends.

- Cut two pieces of cover the size of the ends of the filler.
- Cut enough 1½-inch strips for the welt to reach around both end pieces. For welt cutting and sewing, see page 89, Welting.

2. *Sewing the Bolster.*
   - Sew the welt strip all around both ends. In the event that the seat is to be covered without welt in the seam as in Figure 208, this step may be skipped.
   - Join the large centerpiece of the bolster cover to each end, with the seams between the corners at the bottom.
   - Insert the filler and work the insides evenly all around and in the corners.
   - With a curved needle and heavy thread, sew up the bottom seam (Figure 207).

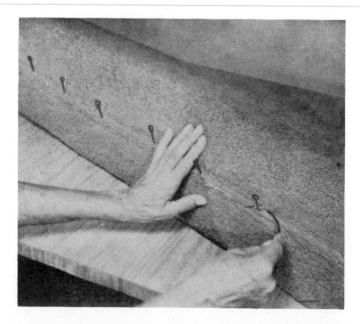

Figure 207. Sewing the bottom seam of the bolster.

Figure 208. Bolster with tapered
ends.

Bolster With Tapered Ends

The tapered bolster is used extensively on Bahama beds (Figure 217). The bolster filler may be purchased ready for covering in either foam rubber of Polyfoam (Figure 209). Since bolsters are available in various sizes, it is best to purchase the filler before cutting the cover. The cover should be made to fit rather snugly over the filler.

1. *Cutting the Cover for the Tapered-End Bolster.*
   - Cut one piece of cover the width of the bolster and long enough to reach around the bolster, allowing 1 inch for closing the cover at the bottom.
   - Cut one piece of cover shaped to the size of the shaped end of the bolster (Figure 210).
   - Lay this shaped end of cover face-to-face on another piece of cover, and cut this out. You will now have a pair of ends.
   - Cut enough 1½ inch strips of cover for the welt to reach around both shaped ends. For welt covering and sewing see page 89, Welting.

2. *Sewing the Bolster.*
   - Sew the welt strips all around both ends. In the event that the seat is to be covered without welt in the seam as in Figure 208, this step may be skipped.

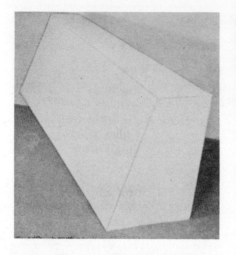

Figure 209. Tapered bolster filler
ready for covering.

Figure 210. Shaped end marked off
on cover.

- Join the large centerpiece of the bolster cover to each end,
  with the seam between the corners at the bottom.
- Insert the filler and work the insides evenly all around and in
  the corners.
- With a curved needle and heavy thread, sew up the bottom
  (Figure 207). When bolsters are covered with a fabric that is
  to be laundered or dry-cleaned frequently, a zipper should be
  inserted in the bottom seam (Figure 211).

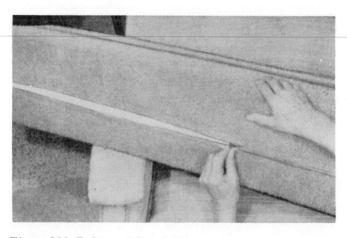

Figure 211. Bolster with a zipper
attached to the bottom.

Figure 212. Bed head-boards covered with plastic covering.

JOB 5. UPHOLSTERED HEADBOARDS

Bed headboards are used extensively on Hollywood bed frames which are made of wood or metal. These frames are constructed for box spring and mattress so that they may be used with or without the headboards (Figure 212).

The legs on the headboards are not made to support the bed. Instead, the headboards are either screwed directly to the wood frame or bolted to the metal frame with the legs of the headboards about 3 inches from the floor.

Since these beds are either twin size (39 inches wide) or full size (54 inches wide), both widths are given here for making the frames as well as for the upholstering.

The most appropriate type of cover for the headboards is the new plastic, Naugahyde (Figure 86), which is available in a number of intricate patterns as well as in a vast variety of colors to harmonize with almost any color scheme.

Constructing the Headboard Frame

1. *Choosing the Wood.*
   - Since the wood frame is entirely covered (with the exception of the lower end posts), the wood need not be No. 1 grained,

but should be fairly close-grained with medium hardness to receive tacks without splitting the frame. Some suitable woods are birch, soft maple, and gum.

2. Joining the Frame.

- The corners may be joined together with glue and flathead wood screws; however, the screws should be countersunk into the wood enough that the heads of the screws will not interfere with the covering. See page 138, Constructing Frames.

Bill of Material

Twin-Size Headboard

Quantity	Description	Dimensions	Part
2	Birch, soft maple, or gum	2 x 2 x 32 inches	End posts
1	Birch, soft maple, or gum	2 x 2 x 39 inches	Top
1	Birch, soft maple, or gum	2 x 2 x 35 inches	Lower stretcher
4	Any suitable wood	1 x 3 x 3 inches	Corner blocks
1	Plywood	½ x 39 x 23 inches	Core

Double-Size Headboard

Quantity	Description	Dimensions	Part
2	Birch, soft maple, or gum	2 x 2 x 32 inches	End posts
1	Birch, soft maple, or gum	2 x 2 x 54 inches	Top
1	Birch, soft maple, or gum	2 x 2 x 50 inches	Lower stretcher
4	Any suitable wood	1 x 3 x 3 inches	Corner blocks
1	Plywood	½ x 54 x 23 inches	Core

3. Assembling the Frame.

The exact sizes of the lumber required are given in the bill of material. It is advisable, however, to cut each piece a little longer. This will permit squaring off each piece before assembling the frame.

- Cut the lumber to size and square it off.
- Join the top piece to the two end posts.
- Join the lower stretcher between the two corner posts. The lower stretcher should be fastened 11 inches from the bottom of the end posts. The distance from the top of the frame to the bottom of the stretcher should be 23 inches.
- Fasten the four corner blocks to the inside of the frame (Figure 213).
- Fasten the plywood to the front of the frame (Figure 214).

Figure 213. Frame construction of bed headboard.

Figure 214. Plywood fastened to the frame.

Upholstering the Twin-Size Headboard

1. *Cutting the Cover.*
  - Cut one piece of cover 46 by 30 inches. The added dimensions permit tacking the cover to the rear of the frame.
  - Cut 130 inches of welt strips. See page 89, Welting.

169

- Cut one piece of lining for the rear, 42 by 26 inches. Since this part of the bed is against the wall, lining such as denim, muslin, or cambric is usually used.

2. *Cutting the Filler.*

The filling should be either ½-inch foam rubber or ½-inch Polyfoam (Figure 146). The filler should be cut so that it will extend over the front edge of the frame, but not over the outer edge, since this would interfere with attaching the welt to the outer edge. Cut the filler 1 inch larger than the frame, all around.

3. *Covering the Headboard.*
- Place the filling evenly all around the plywood.
- Place the covering evenly over the filling. Slip-tack the cover on the bottom, top, and sides to make certain that the lines or pattern in the cover are on straight.
- Stretch the cover to the firmness desired, and then tack the cover to the rear of the frame (Figure 215).
- Lay a pleat at each corner of the frame, with the fold of the pleat laying downward (Figure 215).
- Tack the welt to the outer edge of the frame with the welt extending ¼ inch over the edge.

Figure 215. Laying the top corner pleat.

Figure 216. Blind-tacking the lining to the outside of the frame.

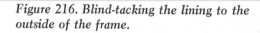
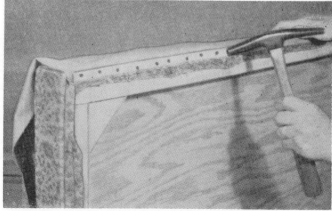

4. *Attaching the Lining to the Outside of the Frame.*
   - With a narrow strip of cardboard, blind-tack the top of the outer lining to the welt (Figure 216).
   - Turn the lining over the cardboard, and tack it to the bottom stretcher.
   - Turn under the sides of the lining and tack or sew it to the welt on each side.

5. *Fastening the Headboard to the Bed Frames.*
   - For wood frames, bore two holes in each leg of the headboard. Screw the headboard to the wood frame, with the legs of the headboard about 3 inches from the floor.
   - For metal frames, bore two holes in the legs of the headboard. These holes should correspond with those already bored in the metal frame. Bolt the headboards to the metal frame, with the legs of the headboard about 3 inches from the floor.

Upholstering the Double-Size Headboard

1. *Cutting the Cover.*
   - Cut one piece of cover 61 by 30 inches to permit tacking the cover to the rear of the frame.
   - Cut 160 inches of welt strips. See page 89. Welting.
   - Cut one piece of lining for the rear, 57 by 26 inches. Since this part of the bed is against the wall, lining of denim, muslin, or cambric can be used.

2. *Cutting the Filling.*
   - The filling should be either a ½-inch slab of foam rubber or a ½-inch slab of Polyfoam (Figure 146).
   - Cut the filler so that it will extend over the front edge of the frame, but *not* over the outer edge, since this would interfere with attaching the welt to the outer edge. Cut the filler 1 inch larger than the frame, all around.

3. *Covering the Headboard.*
   - Place the filling evenly all around on the plywood.
   - Place the covering evenly all around over the filling.
   - Slip-tack the covering on the bottom, sides, and top to make certain that the lines or pattern are on straight.
   - Stretch the cover to the firmness desired, and then tack the cover to the rear of the frame (Figure 215).

- Lay a pleat at each corner of the frame, with the fold of the pleat lying downward (Figure 215).
- Tack the welt to the outer edge of the frame, with the welt extending ¼ inch over the edge.

4. *Attaching the Lining to the Outside of the Frame.*
- With a narrow strip of cardboard, blind-tack the top of the outer lining to the welt (Figure 216).
- Turn the lining over the cardboard, and tack it to the bottom stretcher.
- Turn under the sides of the lining and tack or sew them to the welt on each side.

5. *Fastening the Headboards to the Bed Frames.*
- For wood frames, bore two holes in each leg of the headboard. Screw the headboard to the wood frame, with the legs of the headboard about 3 inches from the floor.
- For metal frames, bore two holes in the legs of the headboard. These holes should correspond with those already bored in the metal frame. Bolt the headboards to the metal frame, with the legs of the headboards about 3 inches from the floor.

JOB 6. BAHAMA LOUNGE

A Bahama lounge is one of the newest styles of modern furniture. Its light weight makes it easy to move if you should want to change the furniture setting in the room.

The most appropriate type of covering for this lounge is either a plain heavy basket weave, a looped fabric, or a frieze in either rayon or mohair. For a more economical fabric, corduroy, rep, terry cloth, or sailcloth may be used.

Although there is no strict rule as to colors for the covering, red, green, and blue are most popular. Personal preference and the overall decor of the room will dictate the choice.

The Bahama lounge is usually made with a loose, tapered bolster for the back, which is covered with the same fabric as that used on the seat. The lounge is not complete without a few toss pillows, covered in a variety of colors contrasting to the basic color of the lounge. For bolster making, see page 163.

Figure 217. *Bahama lounge, upholstered on a solid flush door.*

Bill of Material

Quantity	Description	Dimensions	Part
1	Flush door, solid	30 x 72 inches	Seat
4	Any good wood	12 inches high tapered dia.	Legs
1	Any suitable wood	4 x 50 x 1 inches	Bolster-rest back
2	Wrought iron or mild steel	½ inch dia. x 20 inches	Bolster-rest back supports
4	Steel	10–15 degree angle, size to suit leg diameters	Attaching plates

1. Assembling the Frame.

- Bend the two iron rods 6 inches from the end, and bore three holes through the short end of the rods (Figure 218).
- Locate the center of the door, and screw the short ends of the rods to the bottom of the door 13 inches from the center (Figure 218).
- Locate the center of the wood backrest and bore a ½-inch hole 2 inches deep into the board. These holes must also be 13

Figure 218. *Iron rods fastened to the bottom of the door.*

173

inches from the center of the board, so that the tops of the iron rods will fit into the holes (Figure 220). After the rods and backboard are fitted, remove the rods temporarily so that the covering may be fitted easily.

- Fasten the four angle plates for the legs to the bottom of the door, 12 inches from each end and 3 inches from the front and from the rear.

2. *Cutting the Cover for the Seat.*
- Cut one piece of cover 47 by 88 inches. This size will allow enough cover for all four sides, as well as for tacking the cover to the underside of the door.
- Lay the door on the underside of the cover, equalizing the overhang on all four sides.
- Chalk off the cover all around, and square off the corners.
- Cut the four corner pieces out, allowing ½ inch for seams (Figure 219).
- Sew up the four corners on the cover with ½-inch seams.

3. *Upholstering the Seat.*
- Lay the filler out equally on top of the door. See foam rubber and Polyfoam (Figure 141).
- Strip the sewn cover over the filler, making certain that the cover seams are directly on the door corners (Figure 187).
- Tack the cover to the bottom of the door.
- Replace the two iron rods, using the original screw holes.
- Attach the back bolster rest to the iron rods (Figure 220).

Figure 219. Corners marked off and cut out.

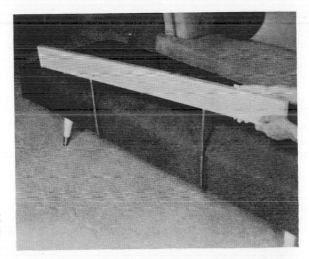

Figure 220. Attaching the back bolster rest to the iron rods.

Figure 221. Sectional bahama lounge.

JOB 7. SECTIONAL BAHAMA LOUNGE

The sectional Bahama lounge has many advantages over the one-piece type. Each piece measures 30 by 24 inches which makes it easy to handle. When the short ends of the sections are placed together end-to-end, the lounge will be 90 inches long and 24 inches deep (Figure 221). When the long ends of the sections are

175

Figure 222. With the long ends placed together, the sectional will be bed size, 6 feet long and 30 inches wide.

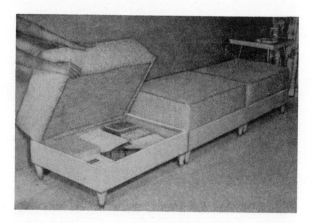

Figure 223. Storage space in the boxing.

placed together end-to-end, the lounge will be bed size—6 feet long and 30 inches deep (Figure 222).

Each section is so constructed that the solid-top upholstery on the seats may be easily lifted out, making a storage space in the boxings (Figure 223).

The most appropriate type of covering for this lounge is either a plain heavy basket weave, a looped pile fabric, or a frieze in either rayon or mohair. For a more economical covering, corduroy, rep, or terry cloth are very appropriate.

If the sectional pieces are made with three loose bolsters for the back, the bolsters should be covered with the same type of fabric that is used on the seats. For bolster making see Bolsters With Square and Tapered Ends, page 163.

If toss pillows are made instead of bolsters, the color of the covering is usually selected to contrast with the color of the seat covering. For toss pillows see page 159.

If the lounge is going to be used much as a bed, it is advisable to cement a 4 inch filler and a 2 inch filler together. This 6 inch thick filler will make a comfortable resilient seat. For filler, see Sponge Rubber and Polyfoam, pages 113-116.

The height of the lounge is governed by the size of legs selected. See Legs (Figure 177).

Since the wood used for the boxing will be exposed, choose a hardwood such as birch or oak. See Frame Construction, page 138.

Although the sizes of lumber given in the bill of material are the exact sizes required, it is best to cut each piece a little longer to allow for squaring off.

Bill of Material (for three pieces)

Quantity	Description	Dimensions	Part
6	Birch or oak	1 x 6 x 30 inches	Long boxing
6	Birch or oak	1 x 6 x 22 inches	Short boxing
3	Plywood	½ x 29 x 23 inches	Bottom
3	Plywood	¾ x 28½ x 22½ inches	Top
12	Quarter round	1½ radius x 5 inches	Corner blocks
12	Legs, with flat attaching plates	Size to suit	

1. *Making the Frame.*
   - Cut the boards for the boxings and square them off to exact size.
   - Cut a rabbet edge (groove) on the inside of each board, top and bottom, ½ inch wide by ¾ inch deep (Figure 224). The bottom plywood fits into the rabbet edge, making a flush surface on the bottom; the top board fits into the groove on top. The top plywood is cut ½ inch smaller than the bottom piece so that the cover may be tacked to the bottom of the top plywood.

2. *Assembling the Frame.*
   - Join the two, side, short boxings to the inside outer edge of the two, front, long boxings. The outside dimensions of the frame should be 30 by 24 inches. Since this boxing will be exposed,

177

Figure 224. Frame completely assembled.

Figure 225. Top covered with welt all around.

Figure 226. Top covered with a one-piece cover.

use wood dowels for joining the ends together or use a dove-tail joint. See Constructing Frames, page 138.
- Attach the four corner blocks (Figure 224).
- Attach the bottom plywood.
- Fit in the top piece of plywood. This piece of plywood should be ¼ inch smaller than the opening all around, allowing the top to fit in loosely after the cover is put on.

3. *Upholstering the Top.*

The top may be covered with welt all around the top outer edge (Figure 225) or with a one-piece cover (Figure 226).

The Welted Cover
- Cut the filler 30 by 24 inches. This size will permit the filler to overhang ½ inch all around the board top. This allowance is for squeeze-out on the filler, as well as to make the cover fit more firmly (Figure 227).

178

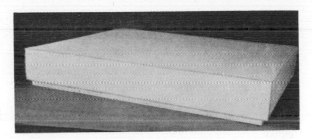

Figure 227. Filler placed on board top.

- Cut the cover for each section in the following sizes:
  Top piece, 30 by 24 inches.
  Two long borders, 31 by 8 inches.
  Two short borders, 25 by 8 inches.
- Cut about 120 inches of welt strips. This amount will allow for joining the strips together, as well as making a connection on the ends. See page 89, Welting.
- Sew the welt all around the top piece.
- Sew the borders over the welt, making certain that the seams on the borders are directly on the corners of the top cover.
- Lay the filler onto the wood top, equalizing the distance all around.
- Strip the sewn cover over the filler, making certain that the seams on the borders are directly on the corners of the board top.
- Tack the cover to the bottom of the board top. Be sure that the welt is the same height all around (Figure 225).

The One-Piece Cover
- Cut the filler 30 by 24 inches. This size will permit the filler to overhang ½ inch all around the board top. This allowance is for squeeze-out on the filler, as well as to make the cover fit more firmly.
- Cut one piece of cover 42 by 36 inches.
- Lay the board onto the underside of the cover, equalizing the distance on all four sides.
- Chalk off the cover all around, and square off the four corners.
- Cut the four corner pieces out, allowing ½ inch for seams (Figure 219).
- Sew up the four corners of the cover with ½ inch seams.
- Lay the filler onto the board top, equalizing the distance all around.
- Strip the sewn cover over the filler, making certain that the corner seams on the cover are directly on the corners of the board top.

JOB 8. PUSH-ABOUT

It would be difficult to name this piece of furniture as it has so many uses in the living room, either as individual cushions, or as a group. (Figure 228).

The cushions may all be made in one color, or they may be made with the same type of covering, but in various color combinations.

As the number of cushions can vary, the directions given here are for only one cushion.

1. *Upholstering the Base.*

The base for the Push-about is a piece of plywood ¾ inch thick, and 22 by 22 inches. The filling should be a 1-inch slab of either foam rubber or polyfoam (Figure 229). The upholstery is simple, and only the corners need to be sewn up after the material is cut (Figure 231).

- Cut the top filler 23 by 23 inches. These dimensions will permit the filler to overhang ½ inch all around the base top (Figure 229). This allowance will provide a squeeze out on the filler, and also insure a firmly fitting cover.
- Center the wood base on the underside of the cover. Then, with chalk draw a line around the base and square off the corners (Figure 230).
- Cut out the four corner pieces, allowing ½ inch for the seams and sew the corners shut.

Figure 228. Push-about.

Figure 229. Polyfoam placed on plywood.

Figure 230. Plywood layed on cover and marked off all around.

- Strip the sewn-up cover over the filler, making certain that the seams on the cover are directly over the corners of the wood base (Figure 231).
- Tack the cover to the bottom of the wood base.
- Tack a piece of black cambric or denim to the bottom, folding the edges of the denim under all around (Figure 231). With wood screws, fasten the casters to the bottom about 1½ inches from each end. (Figure 232).

Figure 231. Cambric tacked to the bottom with the edges folded under.

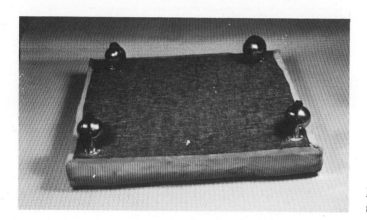

Figure 232. Casters fastened to the bottom.

2. Cutting the Cushion Filling.
The filling should be a piece of foam rubber or polyfoam 4 inches thick and 24 by 24 inches square. These dimensions will provide a squeeze out on the filler, and also insure a firmly fitting cover.

3. Cutting the Cushion Covering.
  • Cut 2 pieces of material 25 by 25 inches square for the top and bottom of the cushion. Then cut approximately 100 inches of welt strips 1½ inches wide. These welt strips may consist of a number of pieces. For making welt, see page 89.
  • Cut out the 4 corners of the material for the top and bottom of the cushion about 2 inches from each end as in Figure 233.

Figure 233. Corners cut out on the cover.

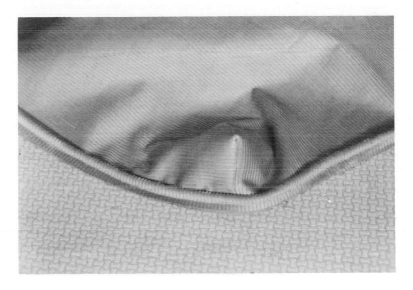

*Figure 234. Welt sewn on one of the
cushion tops.*

4. *Sewing the Cushion.*
   • Sew the 4 cut-out corners shut on both pieces of cushion
     material.
   • Sew the welt all around one of these pieces (Figure 234).
   • Sew the other piece of material over the welt, making certain
     that the sewn-up corners on both pieces of material meet.
     Leave one side of the cushion open for inserting the filler.

183

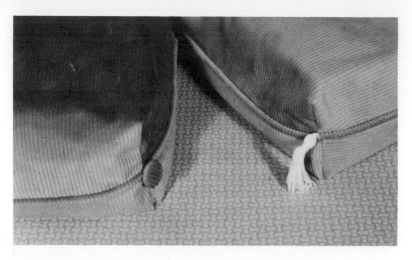

Figure 235. Corners with a covered button and a tassel.

5. Attaching Corner Trim.
- This cushion may be trimmed with either a tassel or a covered button at each corner (Figure 235).
- When tassels are used for the corners, the top ends of the tassels may be sewn between the cushion seams.
- The covered buttons may be sewn directly onto the 4 corners. (For covered buttons, see page 85).

6. Inserting the Filler.
- Fold the filler over carefully.
- Insert the filler into the cover.
- Carefully unfold the filler in the covering.
- With large pins temporarily pin the top and bottom cushion pieces and with a curved needle and twine, sew the opening shut.

7. Inserting the Top Buttons.
- String one button on a piece of twine.
- Thread both ends of the twine through a large upholstery needle.
- Mark the locations for the buttons on each side of the cushion.
- Stick the needle through the marked covering on one side, exactly through to the button marks on the other side.
- String one of the twines to the other button.
- Slipknot the twines together (Figure 236). Draw the twines firmly, and knot them together, so that the knot will be under the button. Then snip the twines off short, so that the ends will be under the button, and will not show (Figure 237).

184

Figure 236. Slip-knots in twines ready to pull down evenly.

Figure 237. Completed cushion on base.

Index